THE HUNT FOR ETHELL GUSH

A low county tale, entangled with
mystery, mysticism, life's failures,
and all enduring faith.

KENDRAL MOBLEY
AND KATHY MOBLEY

authorHOUSE®

AuthorHouse™
1663 Liberty Drive
Bloomington, IN 47403
www.authorhouse.com
Phone: 833-262-8899

Published by AuthorHouse 11/24/2021

ISBN: 978-1-6655-4595-2 (sc)
ISBN: 978-1-6655-4594-5 (hc)
ISBN: 978-1-6655-4606-5 (e)

Library of Congress Control Number: 2021924020

CONTENTS

PRELUDE

The following story is based on true events, though some of the events may not be completely accurate due to one of the character's untimely death. It was written to celebrate the incredible time we shared with our departed friend, "Sister", whom we loved dearly. Out of High respect and love for her, we dedicated our time and our hearts, to give her the graceful completion of her life that she rightfully deserved.

*I*t all began in a small country town, perhaps not too much unlike your own. The name of the town is called Walterboro. It's located in South Carolina's Low Country and unknown to many, an adventure was playing out. The town itself, isn't significant, just your average southern, hick town trying to fancy itself as a tourist attraction, in which most of these small Interstate towns fail miserably. I have often heard many evangelizing preachers, as they visit our lovely city, say they can see old, dreadful spirits perching on the branches like birds or hanging from the trees like moss. Of course, that's if you believe that kind of stuff.

The Edisto river separates Colleton County, where Walterboro is located, from Charleston county. If you were to stand on the bridge that crosses over the Edisto River and look out toward the banks, you would see large, ancient trees with thongs of hanging mosses and all sorts of water birds and water lilies. You would definitely get the feeling of a time long gone. Yep, that's the Lowcountry and its history is rich with stories of love, despair, and triumph. This is one of those stories. It's a story about a couple of simple people that experienced a larger-than-life adventure. I was part of that adventure and here is that story...

Chapter 1

These Old Dry Bones

I was depressed, my husband was on a dead-end job, and my elderly mother had been a teacher, for 30 plus years. Some of her students were handicapped or what some might called mentally challenged. That career was something to be proud of and she had the heart of a servant. That trait led her to constantly act like a servant to the family. For some reason, she felt like the best way to show her love to the family was being the pickup person. Whenever she visited someone's home, she felt the best way to show her love was through her cleaning. This gesture was often rewarded back to her by people saying things like, "she is such a beautiful soul." Her life consisted of robotic, ritualistic behaviors that often led me to believe she had some slight obsessive issue going on. These were not my desires for this loving mother of three. She became a divorcee when I was around three years old. All day long she was at the beck and call of those who needed her the most. Her only comfort came in the late evening as she sat on her couch with a bowl of rice and a cup of tea watching television. This replaced her husband's company, who she divorced years ago. When I was young, she fell on very hard times so at the age of three I was sent to live with my uncle's mother three hours away. We kept in touch and I would spend weekends with my siblings, but I never really lived with my mother again. It was only after ten years of marriage that my husband and I decided to relocate to Walterboro, from Saluda South Carolina, some 145 Miles away. I had come into my mom's life late, so I found that changing her mindset of being "everyone's servant" was challenging to say the least. As with life, whether it be finances, unmet goals or simply life's trials, my own life had become empty, unfulfilled and quite boring. I was slowly falling, spiraling out of control. I felt no excitement in my life and seemed to have no hope for a better tomorrow. Ironically, being the new-comer and a fresh new face, I became everyone's "turn-to" for new hope, brandishing new ideas and a bright smile and thus becoming the center for the family. How I felt seemed to affect everyone else's mood around me. It's a burden when people look to you for hope, but you yourself, have none. There were days of emotional strain and despair because I was faking hope that I did not have. Only in my mid-thirties, I'm not supposed to feel this way. I felt that I should be enjoying life, laughing and doing things with my husband and my two beautiful teen boys. But mostly I watched the gospel shows all day and I pray day and night hoping that some glimmer of light might indulge me. I thought I knew God, but where is He now?

My husband, who is a very good man, was trying hard to be all that he could be for me and the children. I could see his hidden despair and sense of "what's the use." I hid my true doubts and fears so that he could find strength in me. After all, we had been together since we were teens and I loved him. I used to wonder why he never abandoned us; most men would have left years ago. Sometimes I would ask him why he stayed when so many men would have left long ago. With his soft hands on my chin, he turned my face toward his, looked into my eyes, and said, "I love you and I made a promise to God that I would never leave you. I vowed to do what I was called to do as a father and husband." As he spoke, I felt reassured again, but let's be real, how long do you think a marriage can withstand this kind of hopelessness? Such is life and life happened.

One day in the later part of 2004 I was on the couch, watching TV, flipping between Oprah and the gospels as usual. The music went in one ear and out the other. I was dazed, wondering why I couldn't have been like Oprah, rich and famous. The phone rang. It was Mom. She seemed…happily excited about something, which was highly unusual for her. I quickly found out that she wanted me to go with her to a woman's house. Irritated for being pulled out of my fantasy of salvation, I thought to myself, a woman's house? This could easily be a visit to some old person's home, who wants to recant her childhood from the age of 10 to the age of 99. Or the "house" could be the local nursing home and we could end up sitting in a dark room, listening to another childhood tale in a room that smells of medicine. I felt reluctant and did not want to visit anyone! My mood was not in my mom's favor. All I wanted to do was sit on my couch and zone out. But mother was very persistent and would not take no for an answer. As I cursed my way through a quick shower, I had to admit, the excitement in her voice made me curious. Mom finally arrived. I got in the car and we were off. As we rode along, I pouted and thought to myself "this is her big favor for the week from me and my big sacrifice for the month!" We finally made it to the woman's driveway and as mom turned in, I noticed two huge, winged statues of lions, reared on their hinds, claws out and teeth snarling, that left me feeling… odd. I chuckled to myself and

thought, "I hope this isn't a visit to one of the so called "root workers."
As we rounded a curve down the long driveway the house became in
view. It was a large two-story home, hidden away from the main road
by a large grove of pine trees. It was the home I had often dreamed of
having one day as my own, after all, the single wide trailer I had lived
in for over twenty years was falling apart. After parking the car, I took
a couple deep breaths, for I did not know who lived here, or what to
expect, or why I was even here. Who was this woman and why did I
have to come? I guess all my answers would be answered soon. The front
door came open, but no one stepped out.... again, odd. So, we got out
of the car and walked up to the door. From inside the house a gentle
voice said, "Y'all come on in, I will be with you shortly". As we walked
in the house, we noticed that it was filled with old beautiful antiques.
In the center of the dining room was a large eight chair dining table.
The chairs sat high and had high backs like a throne. At the head of the
table was an even larger chair. The room reminded me of King Arthur's
table except this table was rectangle. To one side of the room was a
large, oversized couch and to the other side a massive fireplace. Then
from down the hallway a figure began to emerge. It was her, the woman
momma wanted me to meet. She was tall with a medium build and was
pleasant to look upon with a soothing voice. She walked so softly and
gracefully that she seemed to float across the floor as she walked. She
also carried a very strange looking cane, not that she needed it, I had
learned later that night. It was about five and a half feet in length and
was as tall as the woman. I could tell it had been professionally hand
carved from a tree limb. It had a smooth shiny finish. Noticing how I
was looking at the strange item, the woman explained that her cane was
not for walking, but it was a reminder from God, that He called her to
be who she was, not what other people thought she should be. God told
her to never leave her cane behind. As I let that soak in, introductions

were made. She formally introduced herself as Sarah, but she insisted that we call her Sister. She then offered us seats and took the head chair and began to speak. She talked softly, but intently. I would like for you to remember that I had never met this woman and my mom had only met her two days earlier at Wal-Mart. They had pleasantries and that led to an invitation. Mom told me the woman just seemed different and that was all we knew of her at this point. She looked at me for a second, turned slightly to mom and then back to me and said, "I am a woman of God, and the statues you saw coming in are not evil creatures. They are heavenly beings called Seraphs." I then realized why they had wings. And then, without any warning or hesitation, "Sister" began to make a very peculiar and spectacular proclamation. She said, "You know, you are living in an illusion. The life you are living now is not the life that was intended for you." When I heard this, I was intrigued. For the next two hours Sister talked, proclaiming things that I longed to hear. I was so immersed in her teaching that her words felt like water being poured into a dried-out soul. She talked of riches, glory, vacations, kings and queens, spirits, and devils, political responses, aliens, different dimensions, portals, and accessing spiritual gifts. My jaw dropped, and my mom looked at me with a big grin, as if to say, "I told you so."

Later on, that evening, after Kathy and Ceil are back at their perspective homes, from visiting Sister, Kendral drives his vehicle into his yard. Thank God, he thought, I finally made it home... As I approached the front door, it swung open and Kathy was standing on the other side of the door arms out, smiling with an unusual look of enthusiasm. Then without even saying hello, words began to spurt out of her mouth like fragmented sentences and were accompanied by high enthusiasm. I grabbed her hand, and called out to her, "Kathy!" She calmed down, took a deep breath and began to explain about the woman that her mother and she had gone to see. After sharing with me all of the things this woman had told her, I was a little intrigued. She wanted me to go back with her to see this woman this coming Friday. With condescending resistance, I finally decided to go meet this woman that had gotten her in such a fluster. I was expecting nothing of course. You see, it was not unusual for her to be watching a new product on TV and get excited like a child watching her first SpongeBob cartoon! Anyway, my attitude about the whole thing sprung from love. I just wanted to make sure that she had not fallen into some folly that would consequently lead to more wasted time and mistrust. I must admit though, the person called, "Sister", had her on a high horse because the next several days leading up to Friday, she walked around like she was on cloud nine! It seemed she had found something to hope for. I said to myself. "Kendral, with the mental frustration you always seemed to be in these days, a little hope would do you well." One side of me was praying that this was the light we were looking for to pull us out of life's unmentioned despair, but the other side I was safely clinging to an expected let down.

Chapter 2

KENDRAL

F riday came. It was time for me to go and meet this individual that Kathy and my Mother-in-law, Ceil, had dubbed, "Sister". I guess you could say I had the same unusual feelings Kathy had when she was first invited to go with her mom. I, too, questioned things when I saw the two lion Statues at the driveway entrance. We parked and It seemed like Kathy and Ceil raced to the door. I cautiously approached bringing up the rear. We knocked, and from inside we heard, "Come on in." When we walked in, we were surprised to see two other women there. After introductions, we took seats at the table. Sister, as they called her, immediately turned to me and began to speak. "So, Brother, what's going on with you?" Brother? I took offense quietly; I had not realized that we had become relatives. Jeez, get to know a person first I thought to myself. I replied, "I'm fine." She turned and looked at me with rolling eyes as if she had heard the biggest lie since Nixon and she said, "No, you're not. You are sick and tired of the same old grind day in and day out. You have lost hope and faith in everything." I looked at

Kathy because surely, she had told this woman about me. Then Kathy looked to Sister and asked, "How do you know these things about us if we have not told you?" The two other women at the table chuckled to themselves and said, "She does this all the time. Don't take it personally. It's just a gift she has." Sister continued to drill me, "Brother, don't you know that you are who God says you are? Don't you know that you can speak things into existence? Why do you accept so little when you have been promised so much? Don't you know that God has given you dominion over your ground?" Up until that point I was nodding my head in agreement but then she hit me with a big bomber. "And you also blame and hate God, because you think, He has abandoned you!" Hearing that, my agreeable attitude immediately changed to anger and it began to swell up inside me. I began to tremble with rage at this woman who had no right to judge me. I stood, pointed and yelled, "That's a lie!" She continued to sit calmly looking up at me with glimmering eyes and said, "But it is true, or you would not have agreed to come here." She went on to say, "Do you see any other men here? The Spirit is strong, but the flesh is truly weak. You lie to yourself, but you cannot lie to the Spirit." At that point I began to crumble inside, something was pressing me back down into my seat. I felt ashamed. I began to tear up and soon was weeping. I sat back in the chair and Sister spoke, softly, almost whispering and said, "Quiet, listen. The Spirit is here." Though we were inside, a soft breeze came upon us that made the ceiling fans turn ever so slightly. The room became hazy as if a fog had descended upon it. I had never experienced this before! One of the ladies stood and began to cry out to God, and then my mother-in-law began to chant undecipherable words.

Chapter 3

KATHY

eeing my long-time friend and husband crying like this moved me. I wanted to go to him and comfort him, but Sister grabbed both of our hands, closed her eyes, bowed her head and began to translate the words momma was speaking, "I am here always, seek me and you shall find me." And after she spoke, we all bowed and prayed to the spirit of God that had visited us. Sister explained that the strange utterances coming from Momma, was called speaking in tongues and is also the language of God. She also said, without someone gifted in interpretation of the language it is undecipherable. In certain times God will edify his visitation with a sign like this one. What seemed like an hour had actually been five hours! Everyone was completely drained. Toward the end of our meeting Sister continued to speak about this experience. Sister called this experience the "Glory Zone". It was truly a unique and euphoric feeling. Momma looked ten years younger, we all were refreshed and revitalized. The experience with the Holy Spirit reopened our capacity to believe and rejuvenated our faith in something greater than ourselves. We felt connected to a greater power than we could have imagined!

These types of meetings continued with Sister for months. Now you may be wondering what happened after this praise and Glory Zone experience. Let me explain. One Wednesday night Kendral and I were preparing for bed. The phone rang and it was Sister. She was erratic, requesting us to come over immediately. She said she had something to tell us that was important. Our normal meeting was on Friday or Saturday, so this was unusual. We gathered momma up and went to Sister's house. When we got their Sister was waiting in the yard and requested that we walk around her house seven times praising and thanking God for all His great works. Then she called out Kendral's name, "Brother Kendral, you are a minister and a gate keeper of God's Word. Speak it into existence! Your abusive manager and job are about to come to an end and that pickup truck you wanted is already yours. Receive it!' And he did. Then she called my name, Sister Kathy, you are a prophetess. Your dreams and visions are going to increase. Be aware that this is where all your answers are. Receive it" and I did. Ceil, you are a prophetess, speaking over other people's lives is your calling. Receive it. And she did.

Three weeks later I was home lying on my bed reading my bible when I heard a bump from the living room. It was Kendral, who had been napping on the couch. Suddenly he rose and stumbled down the hall. He entered the room confused and murmuring something about a dream he had while somewhere between sleep and being awake. He claimed that God had told him to get up and go to the car dealer and say these words, "I want that truck", then say no more! Now Kendral's credit was shot. He couldn't sign for a bologna sandwich! Still, he put his clothes on and left. I was shocked because this was not how my husband moved on things. He is the skeptical type. About two hours later, a new blue truck pulled into the yard and it was Kendral. He told me to get in because we needed to go get my car. God had delivered him a new pickup truck! I asked about his bad credit. He told me the dealer saw no issues. We left and as we drove back to the lot to get my car, we said nothing to each other, but I knew that he was thinking the same thing I was thinking. We had tapped into a power that was real and strong! Kendral made the down payment and drove off! Two months later he landed a better job with more pay and only three miles from home. He had previously driven over twenty miles one way to work.

Over the next few visits, Sister taught more and more about powers beyond our imagination and how we could access these things. She said there are negative powers and positive powers. The powers are determined by the deity that you call upon to reach that realm. There are two deities that guard two doors into the same realm. Inside the realm good and evil forces exist. Warlocks and witches use the negative deity, because this deity asks for nothing up front. This deity has many names, but to us he is known as Satan. I mean, it seems with this choice you get all you want for nothing. Seems easy, right? This same deity's technique is to let you get so entangled with this negative power that over a period of time, you are snared and become a minion of his bidding. On the other hand, the deity of light, who we call Jesus, is the other guardian." She stopped, and looked at us curiously, an asked, "You do know that our Lord's name is really not Jesus, right? We, looking dumbfounded, she continued, "NO. Jesus is a translated form of His name. Our Lord and Saviors Hebrew name is Yahshua. He is the Son of the God of Israel." Our nodding heads convinced her that she had taught us the firm truth about the Lords true name. She picked up from where she left off. "Accepting Jesus as your Lord and Savior gives you the key to access the Holy Spirit who empowers the Believer. He is the one that reveals, comforts, guides and protects believers of Jesus. This path requires praise and worship for the innocent life of Jesus given for our sins, with no strings attached. The result is the key to eternal life. No strings attached, and all results are positive. Over the next few months all sorts of positive things happened to me and my mother. My mom, who was retiring, wanted a car of her own. She had been using her sibling's cars for years. God delivered her a new car! I felt overworked, underpaid and depressed at my job. That job closed permanently, and I was able to draw unemployment and became a home keeper which my family loved. It gave me more free time to experience the Glory Zone. Other people that visited Sister received accordingly as their faith allowed. All these things and much more happened within six months of our first visit to Sister's house.

Chapter 4

THE CATCH

A year has passed and the group of eight dwindled to four. We had experienced some of the most miraculous things ever! One Saturday night, early in January, we all were seated at Sister's table. Sister seemed preoccupied. I turned to her and asked what was going on? She took a deep breath and asked a very simple question to everyone; did we love her. We all immediately replied yes. She took another deep breath and told us to look around and notice that God had removed everyone from this group who was not supposed to be there. We started with eight members and now we are four. Also, if you have noticed I have stopped inviting people. She went on to say that the four here now are the only ones able to hear, receive and believe what she was about to say. The Holy Spirit has used me to help you all and now I believe He wants you to help me. I must admit, hearing Sister say, "Now I need your help" I braced myself for something unusual. Sister had always given me the impression that there was something weird running around in her head. From the very start, I had this feeling about her that there was more to her than met the eye. Her husband was a retired minister, and all her children were past their teen years. There are some private details about her relationship with her husband and children that seemed unusual. We figured that because she was so deep into spiritual matters that her kids felt isolated from her. I suspect Sister knew this and tried to bring them into the deep spiritual side, but they slowed her down, so she had to leave them behind. Don't get me wrong, she loved her family, but she had raised her children. They were adults now. She had been a good wife but now it was her time. She let nothing get in the way of that. Sister took another deep breath and with firm calmness in her voice she said, "I believe the woman that raised me is not my biological mother. I believe I was kidnapped as a baby!" I quickly gathered my thoughts and asked her softly, "If you were only a baby how do you know about this? Who told you?" She smiled and said, "In order for you to believe what I have told you so far I had to make sure you believe in spiritual things. That is why for the past eight months we have been seeking out God and his direction through dreams, visions and whispers to our spirits. Now that I know you believe in that; I have no doubt that you can believe that everything I just told you came to me in a dream.

Sister had dropped two massive believe it or not bomb shells on us in less than three minutes! Kendral with his hands covered his face, rubbed his eyes with the inside of his palms and asked, "So, you believe that you were kidnapped when you were a baby. Do you know why you were kidnapped?" Sister looked at Kendral as if exhausted and said, "Brother that is the million-dollar question, isn't it?" I looked at my mother, she was looking at Sister as if to say, "Are you serious?" After a short silence I asked her if her husband and children knew of this. She told me that everyone knew about the dream from immediate family too far off cousins. It dawned on me that the weird feeling I had for Sister, hidden inside of her, was resentment. She honestly felt like her life had been stolen and she was trapped in a life not her own. She then lifted her head and asked, "Do you believe me?" Honestly, we had no reason not to believe her. As a matter fact, this story of kidnapping actually, filled in a lot of holes. For example, the strange distance between her and her husband and between her and her children. Now you would think that a person as close and knowledgeable about Godly things would be very close to her family, but this was not the case. Before she dropped the bombshells, she often would talk about foreign lands as if she had been there before, though she had not. We often wondered why she took up so much time with us. We wondered what she truly got out of us being there for hours on end, but now it all began to come into the light. Her family would not help her nor believe her. She needed friends for support. She believed the Holy Spirit had finally supplied her with true friends, us. We replied without hesitation, "Yes." I then asked, "What do you need from us? How can we help?" Sister answered. "I want to find my real family. It means traveling, phone calls, some computer detective work, and all sorts of snooping, because someone doesn't want me to find my real family. Every time I bring up the subject, I am immediately cast down and portrayed as someone who wants to start trouble. I need your trust to keep what's going on a secret." Momma asked Sister, "Tell us about the dream dear." Sister replied, "In the dreams a lady with a red stone in the center of her forehead keeps coming to me telling me about things that I believe has something to do with my birth. The woman in the dreams keeps pointing at the red stone saying, "So that you will never forget". This has been a recurring dream since I was twelve years old. I don't know the meaning of the red dot on the lady's forehead. The woman in my dream points to her forehead and says "Find Ethell Gush." I believe if I can find that woman, I can get the whole story and maybe find my real family!" Then as if we had thought all the bombs had been dropped that day, she dropped another one. She said, "I am sure you all know by now that my husband and I are not as we should be. He doesn't trust me with his money and because of that I decided years ago to have all my stocks, bonds, social security and retirement checks kept a secret from him and others. I did that because I knew God would send someone to help me. He sent you all. As of right now I have $250,000.00 to find my mother. If it takes every dime to find her, it will be worth it! All I need from you three is faith that I'm not crazy and to believe the story I just told you. The first thing we need to do is find Ethell Gush. Who is Ethell Gush?" I asked. Sister replied, "She is someone that the lady with the red stone on her forehead has told me to find. That is all I know. By now she is a very old lady, but I know this lady is still alive or the woman in my dream would not be continually telling me to find her." She turned to Kendral and said, "I want you to use your computer skills to locate her last known address or anyone related to her. We will start there. I expect you to have some information for me the next time we meet. She turned to me and said, "I want you to be the treasurer." When the time comes, I want you to shop for cheap hotels. The money can get gone quickly!" She turned to my mother and said, "I want you to visit my Aunt with me in the next town. She has information that I need but refuses to give it to me. All I want you to do is to verify that I am not crazy and report what you see and hear to Kathy and Kendral". On the way home we were at a loss for words about what Sister had told us that night. We were excited but a little hesitant to roll over into a full run with Sister. We had to agree amongst the three of us that we should move cautiously with this endeavor. I feared that we might be joining a cult led by a disenfranchised mother and wife. Also, somewhere deep down inside of us we wondered if all this talk about being stolen from parents was just some way Sister dealt with other issues. For example, her husband who seemed distant, or her three children living with her who seemed disinterested in anything she said. In addition, her estranged oldest son tried with all his might to stay as far away from his mother as possible. She loved them all but refused to give in to what they wanted. She felt her entire life was about what they wanted and now that they were all grown up, it was her time to find her real family. We were on board like stowaways on a ship. I perceived that the children and the family saw us as helping their mother slip deeper and deeper into a fantasy. So, we stayed away from saying too much about anything pertaining to "the fantasy" while the family was around. But, when they were away, we would dig in deep, because to us this adventure was what we needed at this point in our lives.

Months passed. Sister had requested Kendral to come up with a plan of what we would need to make our travels safe. Kendral's only request was that we make contacts prior to visiting strange places. We visited many different churches and tent meetings, meeting new friends, discerning spirits, making connections and getting phone numbers from people from many different states. Sister said if we were going to be visiting strange places, we would need to know someone we could call on if we got in a bind. Sometime late in October 2005, we were at Sister's house and she told us that she would be making a trip to Canada and she would be gone for three months. Her daughter was graduating from college and she wanted to be there. She turned to me and said, "Sister Kathy, when I get back, I expect to hit the ground running to find my family." I nodded. Sister caught a plane in Charlotte and for the next three months I collected all the info that we had discussed and put it in a dossier.

Three months later Sister returned as she had promised. We met at the local Cracker Barrel to have lunch. The first thing she asked the three of us was if we had stayed in prayer. The answer came back to her quickly and honestly, "Yes!" She began by telling us that the hunt for her family must start with some information locked away in a closet at her aunt's house. Kendral looked at her with raised eyebrows and asked curiously, "Locked away?" She replied sternly, "Brother Kendral, I don't think you quite understand what is at stake here." (Honestly, other than Sister, did any of us truly know what was at stake?) She continued leaning toward Kendral, her head nodding to show the seriousness of what she was about to say, "My life, my whole entire life has been a lie perpetrated by people who have kept me from knowing the truth because of their own selfish needs. I have had to suffer through it all and pretend to be happy for 53 years! You may doubt me, but you cannot deny the facts!" We looked at her lovingly as she teared up and hugged her. Kendral said to her, "I never doubted you, I was only being cautious as a true friend should be. I love you, Sister." (I love her too, but I was thinking, what facts is she talking about?) As if somehow knowing that it was time for her to lay out some facts for us, she gathered herself and said, "Ok, my aunt, Aunt Rosie, lives in St. George about thirty miles away. Sometimes I ask her about my real family, but she always replies, "Please just drop it. I don't want to talk about that". Sister looked at us and said, "Don't you find that a strange reply?" We nodded slowly. Once I said to my aunt, "Well if you don't want to talk about my real family, may I at least see what you are hiding from me in your locked closet?" My aunt always told me that there is nothing in that closet for me. My question to you is why was it ok for my brother to look in the closet but not ok for me to go anywhere near the closet? If you lived by yourself, why would you have a locked closet, with a dresser blocking the door?" We had no answer. Sister then said, "That closet has what we need to prove that I am not crazy. We need to get into that closet!" I looked across the table at my mother and Kendral. I could read what was on their faces as if it was written in bold ink. It said, "We are not breaking into some old lady's house!" Then Sister said, "I have a way to get the information we need." We were holding our breaths, because nothing that came out of her mouth shocked us at this point and we were sure it had something to do with breaking and entering. She said, "I want us to go and visit my aunt. I want you to earn her trust. She doesn't trust me to wander through her house. The task is simple. After a few visits you will earn her trust. One of you will complain of a bad stomachache and use the restroom. The bathroom is at the back of the house. To get to it you must pass her bedroom with the closet. I know that on Sundays the closet is always unlocked to air out. The dresser that is in front of the door is empty and light, any of us could move it but we women trying to slide the dresser would make too much noise, so Brother Kendral you are the only one strong enough to tilt the dresser and slide it gently and quickly without making a noise. Kendral asked, "What if I am caught?" Sister replied, "You won't be, but if you do, simply say to my aunt that I told you of a strange story and you were trying to prove me wrong." It was late Friday evening. I asked her when she wanted to begin the befriending of her aunt. She said, we will visit her church this Sunday and I will introduce you and she will most certainly ask you back to her house for lunch. We will do this several times; even take her out to dinner as well. Brother Kendral you will need to wash her car or cut her grass, anything to gain her trust. Sister Kathy and Sister Ceil, you will lean to her side on issues as she and I will bump heads. We must be cunning." And we did just that. After four Sundays, and after church lunches at aunt Rosie's house, grass cuttings, car washings, bible studies, and one-sided arguments in which, Kendral and Momma always leaning toward Aunt Rosie's point of view in debates and not Sister's, Sister decided that the following Sunday we would visit her aunt and the final phase of her plan would begin.

Chapter 5

INFILTRATE

The fourth Sunday came, and we went to Aunt Rosie's house to give her a ride to church. The plan was that Kendral was to sit by her on the pew and during service he was to excuse himself several times to visit the restroom. As the plan went into action, Aunt Rosie asked me if Kendral was ok, and I told her that Kendral was dealing with a stomach virus. Aunt Rosie bit the hook like a starving fish and told me that when we got back to her house, she had an old family remedy for that. I smiled at her and from the corner of my eyes I could see Sister smiling, ever so slightly. After service and back at Aunt Rosie's house, she immediately went to work on patching up Kendral with a fresh dose of vinegar and garlic. Afterward and pleased with her nursing, she began to prepare a light lunch. She prepared a platter of ham sandwiches, fresh tomatoes, and cheese cubes, and each of us was given a slice of her homemade cherry pie. Kendral rubbed his stomach and motioned that he did not want anything now and that he would love to take a plate home for later. She smiled and said to him that she hoped he got better soon. As we all sat at the table, Sister began to talk about the church message and before long we were deep into the scripture. Then Sister kicked my leg under the table, and I knew it was time for Kendral to excuse himself. So, I kicked him under the table to let him know it was time for the plan to begin. In Aunt Rosie's home the hallway ran down the middle of the house. When you walk in through the front door immediately on the left is the kitchen area, and immediately to the right is the dining area. If you did not turn left nor right, you would enter a hallway which splits the center of the house. There are bedrooms on both sides and a single bathroom at the very end of the hallway. So, Kendral mentioned to Aunt Rosie he needed to be excused. He then exited the dining area and turned to walk down the hall. From where we sat, we could not see Kendral after he took a few steps down the hall. As he passed by the bedroom door, he looked in and as Sister had said the lock was off the open closet door. He quickly closed the bathroom door loud enough for everyone to hear it but went into the bedroom instead. He slid the dresser and opened the closet door and rummaged around like a kid rummaging through a Lego box very quietly. For a full minute he searched and all he could find of interest was a photo. He took the photo, placed it inside his coat pocket, re-positioned the door and put the dresser back. Suddenly, leaning back in her chair stretching to peek down the hall, Aunt Rosie, asked, "Is your husband OK? Let me go and make sure he has what he needs. I am not sure If I put tissue in the bathroom." Trying to stall her from getting up, Momma placed her hand on aunt Rosie's hand and began going on and on about how delicious the pie was, pleading with Aunt Rosie to tell her the recipe. Being flattered, Aunt Rosie's mind slipped from Kendral to the pie. We were able to stall for a moment, but seconds later she unexpectedly got up and headed for the kitchen. Just as Kendral was turning the corner to come back up the hall from the bedroom, Aunt Rosie turned to look down the hall on her way to the kitchen. As Aunt Rosie turned to look down the hallway, Kendral was already turned to face her as if he had exited the bathroom. We all stopped breathing, and she said to Kendral, "Are you sure I can't get you a cup of hot tea?" Slowly we let out a deep breath. She had not caught him! Kendral replied, "Thank you. The remedy you gave me has already begun to work. I think I will have a piece of that pie please." Aunt Rosie smiled. When Kendral came back to the table his face was sweaty and he looked as guilty as if he had robbed a bank. I said to him, "Are you OK?" He nodded, for he had never done anything like that before. While Aunt Rosie was in the kitchen, Kendral looked at Sister and said, "All I could find was an old photo that might be of some help, so I took it." Sister replied, "That will have to do. Let's wrap this up so we can take a look at it." After the lunch we said our goodbyes. We drove for about three miles before anyone said anything and then Sister asked me to let her see the photo. After eyeing the photo for several moments, she sat back in the seat and went into a deep thought. I asked her if she recognized the photo, she said no. The photo was an old one, a black and white photo of a woman in a knee length dress with a large umbrella over her head standing by a rose bush in a sexy pose. On the back of the photo was the date 1954, and a name, Kala. The first thing we tried to establish was the race of the woman. Why was the race of the woman important you may ask? Well, because in this photo the woman could have been white, Mulatto or native American. If she were white the direction of the mission would be more complicated. I say more complicated because opening old closets reveal hidden things, that desperate people are willing to do just about anything to keep secret. But we did notice two things about her that was interesting and seemed out of place. She had a high bridged pointed nose, and long loose flowing hair. It dawned on me that in the early 50's it would have been highly unusual for a black man to have a photo of a white woman in his possession especially in a pose as sexy as this one. If only the photo had been taken in color, we could have established a skin tone and assumed much. Like I said, we could "assume" much. Not surprising to any of us, Sister began to think that this woman was either her mother or Ethell Gush. How she came to this conclusion, was a mystery to us all. As we drove late that evening, it began to rain. We could hear Sister mumbling, and we could slightly make out she was saying that this photo somehow proved she was right. We finally got to her yard and it began to rain harder. The strain I felt coming from Kendral to question Sister was incredible, but he said nothing. Looking in the visor mirror I pretended to put on some face powder and sneaked a few peeks at Sister. She had put the photo away, closed her eyes and laid her head back on the head rest. My mom broke the incredible silence saying, "So Sister, what do you think?" Sister raised her head, opened her eyes and said, "It's not what I think, it's what you all think"? Surprisingly, Kendral came back with something soft and gentle. He said, "I think first we need to find out who this woman is. If she leads us in the direction, we need to go to find your true family, then we should follow it. If she leads us to nowhere then I think we need to reconsider what we are doing." I could tell that Sister loved the first part of his statement but not the second. Cautiously, she replied, "I believe this photo holds the evidence we need to venture on." I replied, "Then on to finding the evidence that we need. That is what we shall do." The rain stopped, Sister got out and waved us goodbye. On the way home Momma asked us what we thought. I told her I believe the photo should be considered and Kendral agreed. My mom, who tended to usually agree with Kendral, reminded us of what he had said earlier, but agreed with me.

A few days passed. All four of us wondered what to do next. We had a photo that seems to lead to nowhere. Thursday, the day before our usual visit to Sister for prayer and worship, Kendral suggested mentioning to Sister, that we should take the photo to an image specialist that could enhance it. That way we could get a better look at the photo. On the following Friday, we mentioned using a photo specialist and Sister agreed. After prayer, we contacted a local friend of Kendral's who contacted a photographic specialist, and we submitted the photo to him. While we waited for the return of the photo, we speculated on what route to take next if the photo gave us a lead to go further, though I think instead of speculating, Sister fantasized. She never talked as if it would not shed some light and she never allowed us to doubt her. So, before we had any conclusive evidence, we talked as if the photo was already back in our hands. I admit, it was awkward but sometimes having faith in something has an awkwardness to it itself, especially when what is hoped for seemed to be so far away. Later, throughout that night, the four of us pushed further and further down the road of "speculated fantasy" to some light at the end of some tunnel that no one but Sister could see. For the sake of adventure, we gladly indulged.

A week later, on Saturday at 2:00 pm Sister was ecstatic over the phone. Her direct words were, "Can you all please come over? I have good news." So, we got dressed and went over to Sister's house. As we approached the front gate, we noticed Sister was praising and thanking God as she walked around in her yard. We parked, said nothing and joined in on the praise. I had no idea at the time what we were so happy and thankful for, but it's never a bad time to praise God. When we finished, Sister took us back into the house, sat us down and began to ask us if we remembered how she described what the woman in her dream looked like. We all remembered it exactly. The woman in the dream dressed in an Indian style and also wore the cultural red stone in the center of her forehead as you commonly see some sects of Indians today. After acknowledging that, she reached into her bible, pulled out an envelope and placed the original black and white photo on the table. She let a few seconds pass by and then she reached back in the bible and pulled out the enhanced photo. It was a color photo, the specialist had enhanced the original and added color to the black and white, but this photo had many details and to our astonishment the woman's skin was dark, and the woman wore a red dot at the center of her forehead! For what seemed like minutes, no one said a word. Kendral took both photos and held them up to the light trying to find some sign of manipulation but found none. I looked at him and said, "Remember, you chose the photo specialist, not Sister." I think we all were just in a shock. We all realized all of this started with a dream; a dream Sister had of a woman with a red dot on her forehead, who she had never met, coming to her and saying, "Seek out Ethell Gush" and pointing to the red dot on her forehead, saying "So that you shall never forget". Sister with renewed valor, said, "We need to find Ethell Gush!" At that moment I felt like I was in a Star Trek scene, where Captain Picard had made a decision, walked away and the crew was left in the room alone. At the end of the scene, the crew takes a few seconds to stare at one another, waiting for the commercial break.

Silence prevailed. We all were in deep thought. Sister bowed her head as if to pray and so did Momma. I was sitting there with a mind as blank as a new sheet of paper. Kendral paced back and forth alongside the length of the room. I think we all were just trying to organize our next move in our heads. Kendral spoke first and reminded Sister that his attempt at finding anyone by the name of Ethell Gush or just Gush had failed. He stressed to us that he had searched the internet methodically and had found nothing. Suddenly, I remembered watching an actor in a detective movie saying, "The best place to start is at the beginning". As I was remembering it, unknowingly, right under my breath, I whispered it. Sister turned to me and with great enthusiasm said, "That's it!" I turned to her dubiously and asked, "What's it"? "Like you said, we need to go back to where it all began, back to New York. If we could locate the old neighborhood where I grew up, then we may be able to find someone still living there that could point us in the right direction. I will plan a trip to New York. You guys began to prepare yourselves for the trip. We leave in two weeks!" Two weeks into the planning, we received some bad news. Sister's husband had passed away in his sleep. Momma, Kendral and I went to the funeral. We went to the funeral to be there for her if she needed consoling but that was just the thing, she sat there like a statue and no tears came. I guess the unbelief he had concerning her being kidnapped caused a disconnect in their relationship and because of that the relationship became a chilly place on the best days. After the funeral Sister never mentioned her husband again.

Chapter 6

NEW YORK

wo weeks later we landed at JFK Airport, grabbed a taxi and
we were off to find Sister's old neighborhood. The cab smelt like
beer, cigarettes, incense, and last night's club. We must have ridden for
forty-five minutes. We passed skyscrapers and all kinds of municipal
buildings. Soon we went over a bridge and entered lower Harlem. This
area looked very different from the neighborhood we had just passed.
Old row houses greeted us, then came the Projects. At the lower half
of this failed government housing project was what Sister called "Po
Town." At one time it was full of minorities but now it was mostly old
empty dilapidated houses. As I gazed out the window of the decaying
demography, I never understood how the government thought building
houses but not providing jobs for income would add up to equality. This
only led to more crime. After all they only had to look at the failed Native
American Reservation Act, as it had failed as well. Some people still
lived here though. Somehow, they had managed to keep up their home
enough to keep the Department of Social Services or the Department

of Health and Environmental Control from running them out. Sister motioned for the driver to stop and we got out. She gave him his fee and asked him to come back in three hours. We gathered together along the sidewalk as we studied the area for a moment before progressing. Our perspective of the area was from a slight incline, looking downward into a cull-da-sac. I imagined with the evening sun at our backs; how we must have looked from someone's perspective looking out toward us and how Sister's silhouette must have looked standing there in the day with her long cane, long dress and hooded cape flowing in the wind. I giggled to myself. The area was really run down. Kendral pulled me near him and asked Sister jokingly if he should have bought a gun. She smiled and said, "Brother you got Jesus, we don't need a gun". We began to walk down the sidewalk into the cul-de-sac passing by three old houses. At the first one of them, the whole roof had caved in, on another the porch had fallen off and all the windows were broken and the third had major fire damage. Most of the houses in the cull-da-sac were not livable. The fourth house looked occupied, so we stopped in front of it. As we stood there the house door came open and an old man using a walker came out and sat in a chair on the porch. We all took a deep breath and slowly walked up to the fence. Sister hailed the old man with her southern courtesy, and he looked up. He didn't see us at first; he looked over and around us. But then he took his glasses from his face, wiped them clean, replaced them; now finally actually seeing us, he looked directly at us and motioned for us to enter the yard. He then pulled a handkerchief from his pocket, blew his nose into, and placed it back into his pocket. Momma, whispered, "Disgusting."

He asked, "I'm George, how he could help you?" Sister said that she used to live in the old neighborhood and was looking for someone by the name of Ethell Gush. On hearing the name Ethell Gush, the man seemed to look like he had swallowed a bitter bug and spit over the porch railing. He replied, "Got a problem, eh? I guess you need a little something to "healing your ill". I wondered why he put so much emphasis on "heal your ill". The statement came from his mouth like he was disgusted but would enjoy "healing the ill" as he posed it. My question was answered pretty quickly. "Which one of you gals pregnant and don't want the trouble?" (He spit over the railing again as if to show disgust at the name of Ethell Gush). "No need to go a dealing with that old hag. I got what you need right here. I guarantee this will stop the unwanted filth from growing in your belly. Just ask any of the street girls. None of them complain about my stuff." Sister replied, "Nooo!! We are not pregnant and if we were, I would definitely not call it filth! The old buzzard leaned forward, looked at Sister with fake sadness and said, "Well, it would seem to me that if a mother doesn't want her own unborn child, which is her own blood, then to that mother, the unborn child is no more than trash, which is filth." He then leaned back in his chair and looked at us as if he had given us some very wise words. Kendral took a step forward and said, "Sir, like she said, we are not pregnant." The heathen sat up quickly as if to come out of his chair and replied, "We? What do you mean we? Don't tell me you can get pregnant too?" He let out an old dry haggled laugh that left him gagging for breath. When he finally regained his composure and noticed us not laughing, he asked, "So if we "aint" pregnant, then why are you in my yard?" Sister rolled her eyes and said, "We're just trying to find my family and we believe that Ethell Gush has some information that might point us in the right direction. The man acted like he didn't hear that and continued, "You know, I may be able to help you with your ills if you're looking for some other 'special' help." Sister replied sarcastically, feeling insulted, "Like I said sir, we don't need any murdering, we just need information. We only want to know where Ethell Gush is and any information that you can tell us about her". He leaned forward and with

29

straining eyes, for his eyes were deeply greyed from old age, looked at us intently and then eased back in the seat and said, "Well, information doesn't come cheap." "We're willing to pay if the information has some value," Sister said. "All information is valuable. Whether it is helpful or not, you'll pay first, and then you'll get the information. Then you can do as you will with it!" snarled the old bag of bones. So, Sister pulled out twenty dollars and handed it to Kendral and then he handed it to the old man. After the man had smelled and felt the bill, he folded it and put it in a change pouch. The old man's face became rigid, and he squeezed an eye shut as if to examine each of us. "I know of the one you call Ethell Gush. She picked that name up after she came here. Before she moved here, I was told she was called another name. God only knows what her real name is. She was a powerful and well respected "healer" back then. I actually met her on the other side of town. In my younger years I worked at the now shut down East Side Hospital.

I had been employed there for about six months when I first met her. I was a general maintenance person, and she was in the house cleaning department. To her credit, I saw her do a lot of healing in that hospital. Yes sir, a lot of good. There were many days the doctors would say they couldn't do anymore for a patient. Somehow the patients love ones found out about Ethell and sought her out. After the patient's loved ones made a visit to see Ethell," he lowered his voice and winked, 'things changed.' Ethell would pay a late-night visit to the patient's room, and miraculously the next day the patient recovered. Doctors were stunned. Mind you, not all the patients she visited were healed." He smiled an evil grin and softly finished with, "I guess they didn't have enough to pay for her service, or they were not willing to pay the cost of her 'help'". All of a sudden, Sister threw up a hand faced out and asked, "So she was a nurse then?" The old man looked at her and in a scolding voice said, "Are you not listening?!" He turned to me and asked, "Does she have a hearing problem?" Turning back to Sister he continued, "I already told you she was a healer! Calling her a nurse would be an insult to her caliber, I'm sure!" The old fellow slowly leaned back in his chair and silently peered at us. We hesitated for a few seconds and Kendral asked. "Is that it? How long did you work with her and what other kind of healing did you see her do? Do you know where she is now?" The old man looked at Kendral with an upturned smile and asked, "That twenty dollars you gave me, did it come from you or the 'Elder'" there?" He was insinuating that the twenty dollars came from Sister and he was under no obligation to give answers to anyone else. We looked at the man curiously and then back to Momma and then back to the man. (The man was pointing at Sister) Sister, realizing he was talking about her and not like being called an elder when obviously Momma was the older, stared at him with eyes beginning to light up with anger. The old man just smiled at her and said with a soft voice, "The economy is so bad here. Why, a loaf of bread is almost four dollars and a can of coffee is more than that!" Sister's hand went up again and she lifted her voice and said, "Enough! Brother Kendral, Give him forty dollars." She leaned over to Kendral and whispered, "I hope you realize that the hospital he mentioned is the hospital I was born in. You must agree that if this information is correct, it is exactly what we need to find Ethell Gush." Kendral whispered back, "If it isn't, we're out of sixty dollars so far and looking very stupid!" Sister replied, "Faith Brother, Faith!" Sister raised her head and looked at the old man, "First, before we go any further, if a question comes from one of these, (she was waving her hands over us) then assume I have asked the question. Second, if you are deceiving us, surely our God will reveal it to us, and you will have to deal with Him!" I noticed sister said, "our God" letting the man know, we knew was not a believer of the same God we served. Sisters' eyes became like slights. She hissed, "And trust me, you don't want that." The snagged tooth old rascal replied nervously, "Surely the Holy One you speak of will show you the truth and if I am being deceitful, that same one would reveal the lie." The old man grinning now at the money, continued, "Like I said, Ethell was a great healer and I saw her heal when doctors could not." Trying to move the conversation along and get more answers, I said, "Ok, so she healed people. Can you tell us where she might be now?" The older gentlemen replied to no one in particular, "Young people have no patience, but it's your money. I don't know where she is exactly. After the fire of 1948 swept through the neighborhood she relocated for a while to the south side and from there it is rumored that she went back to where she came from." (Silence pursued) We hung our heads in anticipation waiting for the answer to where she came from. "Well?", Sister shouted at the old buzzard. The man said in a low voice, "The Islands." Momma turned to me looking confused and asked, "The Islands?" I turned to the man. "What Island sir?" He replied, "Haiti." At that moment our minds began to fashion together thoughts of voodoo and evil spirits. The old man could see the discomfort and discernment on our faces. Sarcastically he said. "Surely the Holy One will keep you whole." Sister turned away from the man and said to us, "We are finished here. Time to move on." Kendral turned to the old fellow and said, "Thank you Sir, for your time and patience. Is there anything else that you think we should know?" The old fellow squeezed his chin with his fingers and looked down at the ground thoughtfully. "Well, I am curious about why you're looking for Ethell for answers to where your family is? I know she had no relatives here and I you never mentioned you were related to her. I mean, surely you have closer kin that could help you with that. Is there something you're not telling me?" Sister asked him slowly and cautiously, "Do you believe Ethell Gush was capable of doing something illegal for.... (Sister pursed her lips, as if to make sure she used the appropriate words) ...

money?" The old owl grinned with the look of a detective who had just cracked a case that had baffled others. "I believe that people will do just about anything when the need arises, Young Lady. The degree of what they will do is determined by that need. So, yes, if Ethell had seen a dire need to 'help' someone, I do believe that she felt any action that she took was the right thing to do at that time. Ethell was not an evil person, she was a person with knowledge and great understanding of 'strange things.'" "Strange things?" asked Kendral. "Things like what?" The gentleman said, "O, you know, uncanny things, things that most people would call root work or mysticism. But I tell you the truth, I never saw her doing anything without reading a passage from the bible first." "Was she a Christian?", I asked. "I never heard her talk about God or saw her attend a church or funeral. On the other hand, I never saw her do anything that would lead me to believe she was not a traditional Christian," the old man said. "O yea. You may want to go to Gaither Street. There is an herbal store there where she would often pick up her herbal supplies. They may be able to help you, as well. The store is called Halley's Herbs."

From behind us an older lady was slowly making her way down the sidewalk toward us. She waved to us, entered the yard and looking at the old man said "I see you got company, Neighbor! We don't get a lot of that here anymore." The old man just nodded to her. She leaned on her cane and peered at each of us intently, one by one. "I live over there in that red roofed house. You people lost?" Sister looked at her curiously and said, "You look familiar. I think I remember you. I think I used to come to your house and play with your kids." The old woman looked more intently at Sister. "You Buddy's and Elizabeth's girl, aren't you?" Sister nodded. "Of course, I remember you. They called you 'Baby'". Sister blushed, "Yes ma'am." "You were a sweet but feisty little one! All my children, Ron, Derrick and Carol, joined the military. Ron and derrick are retired now. They all live out west. What brings you here child?" Sister got serious. "I'm looking for my family, my real family. I believe that a lady by the name of Ethell Gush can lead me to my real family." The woman cocked her head to one side and asked, "Your real family? What does Ethell Gush have to do with (she hesitated) …Child, What on God's green earth are you talking about? For God's sake, what's all this foolishness about a real family?" Sister told her the short version of why she thought she had been adopted. She purposely left out the part where she thought she had been kidnapped. After finishing, she told the lady, any information about Ethell Gush, would be appreciated. Looking defeated, the woman slowly rolled the name around in her mouth. Then as if a light bulb had come on in her head, she said, "Now there is a name I hadn't heard in years. Ethell and I once work together at the hospital, you know. Yea, we cleaned many bathrooms in that old building. Sure did! She put one hand on her hip, looked up at the old man and said, "I wonder where that old witch is now?" The old man spat over the railing. Sister embarrassingly, asked the old lady what her name was, and the lady told her they all called her Milly. Sister asked Milly, "Do you remember my mother being pregnant with me?" Milly thought for a second and said, "Yes, I remember that well. But I tell you child, during the pregnancy your mother had a hard time. There was several miscarriage threats and we all thought…. well… Thank God. You made it! O Child, even the night you were born was strange. The hospital was on emergency power and… (once again Sister raised her hand and halted the conversation. "You were at the hospital on the night of my birth?" The lady said, "Of course, Child. I was the house cleaner on the 4th floor, the baby delivery ward." Sister looked saddened and said, "So, you can vouch that the woman who birth me was in fact Elizabeth Tolan?" The old man sat back even further in his chair, satisfied that his recollection was supported by Milly's. "I sure can, because I will never forget that night.

It was 1948, and the year of the electrical storm that knocked the Midway Power Plant out which supplied electrical power to the East side. (She pointed to the old man as he nodded in agreement remembering that horrific storm.) Milly continued. "Like I said, the hospital was without power and running on generators, so the lighting was low. I was just finishing cleaning a bathroom and was headed down the hall to the housekeeping supply room when I saw that the elevator door was slightly ajar. There was a nurse at her station pushing buttons trying to contact the other floors to no avail. You know, when it's low lighting, your eyes play tricks on you. Shadows play in the light of the long hallways. Well, you see, that dreadful night I thought I saw Ethell on my floor, which was uncommon because each housekeeper had their own specific floor to attend. I did not care much for her, so I wondered why she was on my floor. She had come up using the stairway because the elevator wasn't working. She headed down the hallway. I figured she was going to do one of her so-called miracle cures, that George has probably already mention to you." (George nodded in agreement that he had) "So, I watched her as she stopped outside the window where she could look in at the newborns. I chuckled to myself, saying, "Old Girl, you can look but you should have had your own when you were younger!" I turned and walked to the supply room. Once I got my cart resupplied, I exited the room and noticed a nurse removing a baby from the viewing room. She headed to the feeding room where a mother waited to feed her baby. I watched the nurse as the door to the room opened." Sister asked, "Did you ever have a conversation with this woman, I mean, the waiting mother?" "No, why would I? She was so reclusive and never had visitors at all. Anyway, your mom was in a birthing room that night and from the commotion that was coming from the room I figured she was giving birth to you. As I passed by the room I peeped in and there stood your dad holding you. You were such a beautiful child!" We heard a honk from a cab driver. Sister looked at the lady humbly and said, "Thank you for your time. You have been most helpful to me." (Sister took out a pen and wrote her cell phone number on the paper and handed it to the lady). "If you're ever in South Carolina and can remember anything concerning this issue or if you ever need someone to talk to, call me." The woman took the piece of paper, folded it and tucked it away in her bra. We said our goodbyes' and we were off to Gaither Street.

Chapter 7

THE HERBAL SHOP

When we got to the location, we found that Halley's Herbs was still in business just as the old man had said. We stopped the driver and went in. The store was set up strangely. Walking in you could only proceed directly to the counter at the back of the store. This was the only way to access the aisle if you wanted to browse. The aisle was narrow. At the counter was a young girl with two long braids leading down her back. She was around the age of thirteen. Sister asked, "Is there an adult here that I might ask a question?" The girl stared for a moment looking emotionless. Then she turned her head over her shoulder and shouted, "Granny!" From beyond a beaded curtain, we heard a drawer close and a chair sliding. The sound of bedroom shoes sliding across the floor was heading our way. As the lady appeared through the curtain, she touched things for support. She was a short heavy-set woman with blue dye in her hair and she was blind or at least visually impaired. When she made it to the counter, she put both hands on the counter and said, "Greetings. How may I help you?" Before we could speak, she said, "Wait. You're looking for someone. Someone from your past. A woman. You believe she can help you with something. Am I correct?" Kendral leaned over to me and whispered, "The old man or woman probably called ahead and told her that information." I nodded in agreement. Sister floated up to the counter with the grace of a swan and said, "Yes. You are correct. We are looking for a friend from long ago by the name of Ethell Gush." "And you say Ethell Gush was a friend of yours?" the lady questioned. Sister replied, "Well, she was a friend to some of my family years ago and I am trying to find her to find out what happened to my family." Who was your family?" the lady asked. Sister replied, "I am a Tolan, Sarah Tolan is my name". "Were you related to Buddy Tolan?" the lady asked. Sister replied, "Yes! That was my father." "Awww, I see. Buddy visited my shop a lot and so did Ethell. Your mother, what was her name?" Sister replied, "Well, that's complicated." The old woman straightened her shoulders and said, "Complications are questions that need answers, I'm sure." Sister, hesitated and then gave the woman the name of the lady who she thought was not her biological mother, "Elizabeth Tolan." Halley repeated the name slowly and replied, "Naw. I can't place her name, but I met her several times. Of course, I never could figure out her strange accent. She said she was attending the medical school and worked part time as a candy stripe at the hospital." At the mention of the word accent, Kendral nudged me. Sister asked, "Excuse me, but I notice that you are visually impaired. How long have you been this way?" "Since birth," the lady replied. Sister questioned, "Then how do you know this was my mother?" "The lady smiled saying, "Because Buddy told me she was!" Sister replied, "But my mother never went to medical school nor did she ever work at the hospital. In fact, she could not stand the site of blood and my mother did not have a strange accent." "I'm confused then. Did he remarry?" asked the old lady. Without answering, Sister asked, "Do you remember what year this was when they began coming to this store together?" The old lady said, "It must have been around 1945 or 1946, because I can remember when all electrical power went out from that bad storm and that was in '48." "Do you remember what they purchased when they visited you?" asked Sister. Sarcastically, but nicely, the old lady said, "Now I'm nowhere young as I used to be and that was many years ago. No, I can't remember." After a few more questions and buying small trinkets to keep the conversation going, we found out the lady's name was Grace, Grace Halley. Finding out that the woman Grace met was not the woman Sister was told was her biological mother, gave Sister new strength. For the next ten minutes as we shopped in the store, Sister continued to drill the woman with more questions. I thought to myself and I am sure Sister was pondering this as well, why would her dad bring some pregnant woman to this shop, a woman he called his wife, a woman that had an accent and a woman no one else seems to have known about. After all, no one had mentioned anything about a family member with an accent. Off to the side of the store I watched Momma motion for me and Kendral to come to her. When we got to her, Momma was at the back of the store peering through beaded curtains into another room. Sister was in conversation with Grace, so we were left unattended and decided to be a little nosey. Moving ever so quietly we eased through the curtain without making a sound. We weren't sure if this part of the store was for buying customers or just a small room for storage. But like I said, we were curious. As we entered the room, the lighting was bad. A forty-watt light bulb was trying frantically to light the whole room but was straining to do that! There were six rows of shelves. On the shelves were jars of different types of preserved vegetables and fruits. There was nothing unusual about that. After all, this was an herb store. However, being with Sister for the past year had taught us how to recognize when the Holy Spirit was proactive in us, and at the moment it was urging us to go further into the room.

As we walked further into the room the smell of the room became mustier. This suggested to me the deeper we went in, the deeper underground we descended. This also meant this part of the building was hidden from the outside. Looking at the building from the outside you would never know there was another part to the structure. I went left, Momma kept straight and Kendral ventured to the right side of the rows of aisles. What little calmness we had, crept away when I heard Kendral say in a strange frantic tone, "What in the world?" I turned and walked toward him as quickly as I could. I rounded the corner to his aisle. By that time Momma had caught up with me. When we finally got to him, he was staring at us blankly! I looked at him and touched his face gently and said, "What is it? Are you okay?" He pointed to the jars alongside the right of me. As we turned, what we saw shocked us and made us very queasy! Along the entire wall were jars of different sizes. Inside each jar was some sort of animal in its early form of gestation floating in formaldehyde. You know, there are certain moments when a combined sigh of relief is needed. This was one of those moments because we were generally relieved to see animals and not human embryos in the jars. After shaking off that horrible mind tease, we giggled to one another, ashamed at being frightened of animal embryos. We took a few moments to gather ourselves. Then I noticed to my left another row of shelves covered by a curtain. Momma and Kendral sensing my building anxiety, looked at each other and then we all turned our heads at the same time toward the left side of the row. The whole side was covered by a curtain from top to bottom. Now, keep in mind these shelves were taller than Kendral, who stands about six feet. In fact, I would say the top shelves were a least seven-foot high! Each shelf had five dividing shelves from the top to the floor and each row was about twelve-foot long. I knew what Kendral was thinking. The way he was looking could not be hidden, "Do we look behind this curtain or do we just walk out now and leave well enough alone?" Momma spoke up. "Now, Brother, you know we have to look. That's why we're here and you know Sister would be ticked if we didn't." He nodded and slowly peeled back the curtain to one side. What we saw was a horrible site! The thing we hoped not to see, we saw! Have you ever gotten that feeling that you had uncovered something done by a criminal? And if the criminal knew you had uncovered it, he would never let you leave alive? Well, that was this moment. I felt like running! In each jar from the floor to the top shelf was our worst fear. Each shelf had a jar all the way across. Each shelf contained different stages of a human babies' growth! One had an embryo, the other a fetus and the third a full-size baby in it! On each jar was a label, giving the sex, race, age and year of preservation. I was appalled and Kendral went to a corner and vomited! Once he gathered himself, he returned, touched my shoulder and grabbed Momma by the elbow and asked us to follow him out of the room. But I did not move. I was truly in shock. Something about the specimens caught my eye. I thought I had seen the worst of it, but then I also noticed prices on the jars. Not only was there a price for the whole jar, but there were also prices for individual parts of what was in the jar! So, not only were the whole specimen for sale, but parts were for sale as well! As I pointed that out, our minds began to turn like grinding gears to speculate the objective here. What kind of person and what kind of business would have such a sinister and ungodly service? What kind of human could cut up a baby like a chicken and sale individual parts??? Kendral broke us out of our brain turmoil and whispered to us that we needed to get the heck out of the room and report our findings to Sister. We agreed and quietly walked back to the main room. Sister was still in conversation with Grace and as we walked back up the aisles, we picked up some herbs, thanked Grace for her time and went outside to the cab. On entering the cab, Sister stared at us with intent and said, "Well, what did you perceive about this woman?" None of us looked at her. Finally, Momma began to speak to her about the jars in the room. Surprisingly, Sister was not shocked. On hearing this information, she seemed to solve a mystery only she had thought about. She simply nodded her head and mentally filed that information away. Kendral looked at Sister with searing eyes. "Shouldn't we go back in there and confront this woman?" Sister turned to him and said, "To what degree? Are you going to arrest her 'Officer'? Are you going to accuse her of witchcraft and burn her at the stake? Or maybe you want to get Channel Six News down here and for fifty bucks ruin any chance of future information from this woman? Finally, sadly she said, "Those babies in those jars are already dead. There is nothing we can do about them, at the moment, that we can't do later. I suspect she got them from that heathen George. No, we are doing nothing now. One mountain at a time. The most important information thus far was establishing that Milly, George and Grace dealt with Ethell Gush. Grace also knew my father and his mysterious side woman who she claimed had an accent of unknown origin. We have established that there is some very disgusting underworld business going on here and I attend to turn every doorknob to find my family!" Kendral became enraged and shouted back across the cab, "Did you not hear what we just said? Do you realize what that haggled old witch of a woman had in her backroom? Let me repeat it then! It looked like babies in jars. She is probably cutting up babies and selling them piece by piece for use in some kind of voodoo, black magic crap! Does that mean nothing to you? I thought as Saints of the Most-High God, we were supposed to uproot and come against all evil." I reached over to calm him, but he brushed my hand away. "Furthermore, at what point do we find ourselves just as guilty as the accused if we do nothing?" He ended his ramping and fell quiet. Sister looked at him with a straight face. With the confidence of a lioness and the wisdom of an old owl, she replied softly, "Brother, I understand your feelings right now and I promise you, when we have what we need we will bring the full force of the Holy Spirit and the Law against this woman and her business. That I promise you. But for now, we need her. We do not need to let her know we expect anything because we know that she has a connection with Ethell. There is a more sinister connection here, I can feel it in my spirit. I attend to find out what it is and bring the full extent of the law and God to bear!" Still fuming, but slowly realizing that Sister had made some good points, Kendral began to relax, but he was far from happy. With that the car fell silent and we all stared off into limbo trying to think about what we had learned today.

My thoughts trailed off as well. I was in the front seat and looked around at the faces in the cab. Everyone was in deep thought. How I wish I could read minds at that moment. I wondered what Momma actually thought about all this. Momma was an energetic sixty-eight-year-old, but the trip was exhausting on every level both physically and emotionally. But, to her credit, Momma never complained, not once! How was this hunt for Sister's family affecting the rest of us? I thought about what Kendral had said about the weird old lady, Grace, calling her a witch. What if she was actually a witch and to what degree did her magic work? Could she turn us to toads? Could she have somehow manipulated us and made us think exactly what she wanted us to think and send us on a wild goose chase? But, then again, I had to remember Sister's determination. Wild goose chase or not, Sister would overturn every rock, even if it only gave the slightest speculation of truth about her real family. We finally made it back to the motel and followed Sister up the stairs. My full intention at the moment was to get as far away from the crowd as reasonably as I could. I wanted to go to my own room, shower, wrap myself in my comfort blanket and get Kendral to hold me close. But that didn't happen. As we climbed the stairs to the second floor, we followed Sister right into her room, bypassing our own. This must have been our minds saying unconsciously, "we need togetherness." We all took seats around the room. Sister sat on the couch by me and Kendral was across the room on a stool. Momma was in the bathroom washing her hands. My face must have shown worry and it must have shown me to be in full question mode. I was quite emotional. I wasn't sure if I was going to cry or go into a rage. What the heck was wrong with me? Then, as if the doctor had ordered it, a soft, gentle hand laid upon my knee and Sister began to speak, "I want to go over what we have learned today. I perceive you all have missed a very important piece to this puzzle. I can tell you all are full of questions and have difficulty seeing through this. First, let me ask you this, "Do you have any doubts that there is something strange going on here?" We nodded our heads in agreement. "From the information we have attained today, is this enough proof for you all, especially you, Brother Kendral, to proceed? I think Kendral was a little embarrassed at this finger pointing, but he realized that he had been the biggest doubter of the group. So, smiling he said, "I must admit, there is something going on here, but I do not know what this information is suggesting." Sister replied, "Exactly! There is room here for much speculation and there is room for my story of my lost family to be true as well. Is it not?" Sister slowly looked around the room to read the faces of everyone. We all nodded our heads. "Good. Since we are all in agreement on that, I now can go ahead and tell you what I speculate from the information we have thus far." (Honestly, I was asking God for someone in this group that could bring all this information overload together and give some direction on how to proceed. Whenever Sister was in her teaching mode her eyes would close, her hands would fold together, and her voice would change to an intense but softer tone. The room became completely silent.) She began, "We now know that Ethell Gush is actually a real person. Before this, she was just a fragment of, "crazy Sister's mind" she said sarcastically." We all grinned sheepishly. "We know something else that is powerful toward my cause. We know that Ethell Gush and the woman that raised me were at the hospital at the time of my birth. (I noticed that Sister no longer called the lady that raised her by her name but only mentioned her as, "the lady that raised me.") She asked us. "What about the strange behavior of Ethell Gush at the hospital that night on my birth?" She looked at Kendral and he nodded his head. She continued, "I am very curious about this woman with the accent. There seems to be no lead on where the woman with the accent is today. The only person that can settle this is still the very person we haven't found yet, Ethell Gush. I have come to suspect that Ethell is more than just a healer or simple root worker. I believe that she is a top tier warlock." (Sister was saying all of this in the same demeanor as a preacher would shout out, "God is alive!") "If Ethell is what I suspect her to be, we need to prepare before we meet her because I am sure that when we do, we will need the full armor of God with us. Kendral looked up from his hands and asked, "What do you mean, 'when we meet her?' We don't even know where this woman is." Sister looked at him with a look of pure intensity and said, "Of course we do, Brother. Ethell is in Haiti, and that is where we are going to hunt her down. She is going to tell me what she knows about the night of my birth and what information she has about my family!" I tell you the truth. There aren't many people who can stare my husband down or match his resolve. But with Sister, he had definitely met his match and he knew it! The strange thing about that was, he loved it. I think he just liked the idea of someone else taking the lead besides him all the time. The next day we caught a plane, and we were soon back in South Carolina. Sister told us to get some rest then to take the next couple weeks to prepare for our trip to Haiti. About three weeks later she asked if we could meet her on Friday at her house around seven p.m. We agreed.

Chapter 8

MR. LATE EVENING

F riday finally came. Evidently, we got to Sister's house a little early, for no one was home. It wasn't unusual for Sister to run out to get goodies from the country store right before we arrived. So, Momma, Kendral and I waited patiently in the car for her to return. Ten or fifteen minutes must have passed by. Then we noticed a large black Tahoe SUV with very dark tinted windows slowly coming down the driveway. It parked across from us, facing us. The sun was at our backs so as the sunlight hit the Tahoe's windshield, we were partially blinded. We did not recognize the vehicle. As we sat there, Sister finally arrived and parked. She grabbed some bags from the car seat and went into the house, never acknowledging anyone else was in the yard, but her. Kendral watched as she twisted the doorknob to go in and he slowly shook his head. Though he was right, she could be a little eccentric at times, I ignored his notion and pretended not to notice her. We got out of the car, grabbed our bibles and walked toward the house. As I walked toward the house door, I glanced over to the SUV to at least give a friendly smile to its occupants and to be inviting, but still, I could not see into the vehicle. Walking into the house; I greeted Sister and found a seat. Sister's big dining room table was laid out with all sorts of goodies. Like I mentioned earlier, the table had eight high back chairs that sat a person high off the floor. In fact, they made you feel like you were sitting on a king's or queens' throne! At the head of the table was the larger chair that often-only Sister would use. Today though, she sat in a chair near it leaving it empty. We seated ourselves and immediately began to praise and worship. The Holy Spirit began to move to-and- fro among us. We all needed that badly. Our spirits were refreshed as we all came on to one accord. I felt re-energized. We all did! You know, you can praise God alone, but there is much power in a group! With our eyes closed, and heads bowed, our tongues spoke the language of God in intercessory prayer as we gave thanks to the highest God! And then as the Holy Spirit began to release us, we came to ourselves and slowly sat back in our seats, ending the dancing and shouting for God. I was about to ask Sister about the SUV outside when a cold chill ran over the room. I shimmered as a tickling feeling ran down my back. Then we heard a knock on the door and Sister shouted, "Come in!" But the door never opened. Kendral got up and went to the door but when he got there, he stopped in his tracks and just stared at the closed door. I don't know what went through his mind, maybe the earlier chill that ran down our bodies, caused him to hesitate.

For a moment he seemed fearful. What or who was on the other side of the door? Recognizing his hesitation, Sister got up, walked over to him and put her hand on his shoulder. "I got it, Brother". He turned and walked back to his seat. She opened the door, but no one was there! The SUV was still in the yard, yet no one was at the door! We all stared at the empty passage that led from us at the table, past Sister and into the yard to the SUV. Then from behind us came, "Greetings!" in a voice that seemed old and toothless. We turned in horrid shock. In the king's chair sat an old bald man dressed in a large black fur robe and brown fur hat. A younger man was standing behind him helping him to remove his robe and hat. "I hope I didn't miss anything," he said. Now, I am sure the same thought that was on my mind was on everyone else's mind…How in the world did these men get past us? We never saw them come in. Sister gathered herself from shock and said, "I would like for you to meet Mr….. Sister turned to the man embarrassingly and motioned for him to say his name. He stood upon trembling legs, with a cane and the help of the man standing behind him. He bowed and said, "My name is Evening, Mr. Late Evening, but please call me, Evening." I thought Sister's cane looked old and weathered but this one looked like it came straight from the set of Lord of the Rings! Kendral leaned over to me and whispered, "Excuse me, but did he just say his name was, Late…. Late Evening, like "late in the evening?" I ignored him because the man was looking at Kendral with a straight face that asked, "Do you have a problem with my name, Son?" Kendral sat up a little straighter and smiled at the man with a guilty look on his face. The old fellow was short, no hair and his face was hairless except for heavy eyebrows that swept away from his face. The eyebrows were pure white and arched high making him look wise. He sat back down, and silence came over the room. Sister broke the silence, cleared her throat and said, "Earlier I had mentioned to you that we needed to prepare ourselves for the visit to Haiti." We nodded. "I have invited Mr. Evening here to help us prepare for what is ahead of us." Kendral said, "I have been to places like Haiti before. Why is this trip any different?" The old man raised a finger and said, "Because when you went to these places earlier you were not in warfare with spirits. Believe me when I say you are searching out more of a spirit then a person and you are most definitely at war! This spirit does not want to be confronted on your terms. It wants to confront on its own terms. So, every spirit under its control will be compelled to hide the high spirit and mislead you in every subtle way. That is why I am here, to show you how to keep from being misled. I have been assured by the lady of the house (he was referring to Sister) that you all are aware of the workings of demonology and such?" We nodded. Mr. Evening continued, "Though I perceive the person that you are searching for is not a demon per say, however the Jars you found at the Herbal shop suggests a coalition of dark arts at work." He explained to us that humans who use dark arts give demonic forces certain freedoms to be able to act in this world and in return the demonic forces give the human special abilities. As for demons, they can best be described as the dark arts manifested. They are essentially dark art. Me, I have been assisting the "Way" for a long time. My mother and her mother did this as well. As far as I can tell, my blood line suggests that my ancestors come from the eastern hemisphere. The "Way" was the old term used by the ancient Hebrews to hide that they were actually Christians converted during the time of Christians persecution by Rome of ancient Israel. For the next four hours Mr. Evening asked questions, answered questions and taught us the ways of the wicked.

This man was so versed in dealing with evil spirits that I wondered if he himself wasn't some kind of war lock. He told us of things that he had witnessed over his lifetime. We were spellbound and some of the stories were hard to believe. We learned things we thought were ordinary happenings were really dark principalities positioning themselves in high places. He told us about some of the political, religious and social leaders who dealt in the dark arts for the kingdom of the "Evil One". I asked him, if he knew all of this, why hasn't the Church come against these demons?" He replied, "Because these things must be. When sin came into this world, it preordained certain things must happen. The church can only help guide the path of the elect, help to reclaim the backslider unto God. Things predestined to fall will fall and things predestined to rise shall rise. Remember what Christ said. He did not come to save the world but to save those who would believe in Him. Yes, we should be very aware of what is going on around us, but we need not concern ourselves with things preordained by God, things that must happen. For those things we cannot change. Now I have helped you all that I can." (Through this whole ordeal the man standing behind Mr. Evening never moved. He just stood there motionless.) Then Mr. Evening asked. "May I use your restroom?" Sister nodded to the hallway and Mr. Evening with the help of his helper put his robe and hat back on and went to the bathroom. When he had left the room and we were sure he was out of hearing distance, Sister leaned toward the group and whispered softly, "I would ask Mr. Evening if he knew Ethell Gush. Do you think I should?" "Why would he know Ethell Gush," I asked inquisitively? Before Sister could give an answer, Mr. Evening was heading back to the table. This time though, he did not sit. He stood at the head of the table as if waiting for something. At that moment, Sister took the opportunity to ask the question. She began, "Mr. Evening do you know Ethell.... (before Sister could get out another syllable, Mr. Evening bought his two hands together to make a loud clap. To our shock, he slapped his helper so hard that the helper spun around and passed out on the floor! We all quickly came to our feet in disbelief and then before we could protest, Mr. Evening said, "You must never say her name in my presence unless I have created a cloaking shroud to hide myself! Now that the shroud is up, we have but a few minutes to discuss her. Yes, I know of the one whom you speak. She is like me, of the highest order of our Covenant, but her way of doing things, well...the order could not allow. She was removed and now is independent of the Covenant's resources. Understand, this puts her at a grave disadvantage so to survive she dwells in any type of doings, good or evil." Kendral asked, "You said that she was of the same order as you, which I infer you meant of "The Way" but she was kicked out? You also said that you help those who are of "The Way"? You are of "The Way". Surely you can control her because she too was of, "The Way"? Could you at least force her to tell the truth about Sister's family?" Mr. Evening glanced at Kendral and said, "Ethell Gush made a deal with the Covenant and as long as she does not break that deal, she can do as she pleases. The deal was, that she must never take a life, and never assist any soul to damn itself. For that reason, I cannot interfere with her and she must never know that I have assisted you. And as to where she is, I do not know and if I did it would be a breach of contract to tell you. But I can tell you this, she already knows you seek her, and she also knows that if you can prove that she had anything to do with you being taken from your birth mother that would be a breach of the contract. If you can get her to confess dealing in this manner, I can act. I can act on the behalf of the covenant. So, she will not be found easily. When and if you do find her, you will have to be cunning to get her to confess her part in the matter. Around that time the helper man had begun to stir. Mr. Evening took a few slow steps backward and put his finger to his lips making a shhh sound and whispered, "The cloak is ending." Kendral leaned in over to me and whispered, "Sooo...The clap was to evoke the spirit that controls the spell. The slap making the helper pass out was to begin the cloaking spell and the stirring of the helper ended it...... something like a human hourglass.... interesting." I looked annoyingly at Kendral, because while his attention was on the method, my concerns were on that poor man Mr. Evening had slapped. He was still trying to get his bearings and stand on his feet.

A few seconds later he was back at Mr. Evening's side as if nothing had happened. I could see the look on Momma's face and tell she wanted to challenge Mr. Evening about slapping his helper. She most assuredly thought that was absolutely deplorable. I put my hand on hers to calm her and she relented. After gazing at the group, Mr. Evening said "If all hearts are at ease and minds are clear, may we pray? Then I will kindly be on my way. I have another engagement tonight." In acknowledgement, we all bowed our heads to pray. Mr. Evening told us he would start the prayer then the person to his left would say a few words and Kendral should end it. As suggested, he started, then Momma took her turn. After her, I took my turn and from there, Sister. Kendral finished with an Amen. This would have been an ordinally prayer, if not for the fact that when we opened our eyes, Mr. Evening was gone and so was his helper. It was as if he had never been there! Kendral got up and was taking a step to the door to see if Mr. Evening was still in the yard, but Sister stopped him. "What's the use, Brother? He is gone." Momma looked at Sister and asked her how he did that. Sister could only shrug her shoulders and reply "We've seen strange things and I do believe stranger things are yet to come."

It was late and we all were tired, so we decided to end the night. We went home and went over all the things we had heard that night. I had kept a notebook full of a lot of things we had learned. I decided to look back through at the notes, just to make sure we had not missed anything, just as Sister had asked me to do. My conclusion was that everything we had learned so far did indeed seem to lead us to one conclusion. That conclusion was that Sister's story of a missing family seemed more real each day. However, I was not going to discuss any of our opinions without Sister being present. I was not going to give the devil any help in defeating us by separating us on the topic. Sometimes giving the enemy a chance to gather himself after getting him down can lead to an unforeseen comeback on his part. Besides, I knew it wouldn't be long before Sister was calling us up with the same conclusion. I also knew that at this point in our search, we had come to the tilting point.

If anyone had any doubts about going forward, now would be the time to voice that opinion. Completing my thoughts, I realized anyone doubting had better have their facts together because I was sure Sister was completely submerged in "her" facts going forward. A few days had passed. The weekend came and went. It was strange for Sister not to call and Momma was worried about her. So, we decided to call, and sure enough Sister picked up the phone. "Hello", she answered. After a sweet hello, she quickly changed gears and became accusatory. "Sister Kathy", she said, "Did you go over your notebook with your momma and husband?" I replied, "Yes, of course." "Well, it's been a week or more and no one has called me about anything. Is there a problem?" I replied with a slow, "Nooo." From the tone in her voice, I realized that what I had suspected was coming to life. She definitely realized what I had realized. We were at the tipping point; or in her case, the no going back point and she wanted to extinguish any doubters. She asked, "I am certain that you all have come to some conclusion on the next move, if any move is to be taken at all? (That didn't sound like a question to me. It sounded more like a statement disguised as a question) "Do we move on the information we have gained, or have we come to a place where we need to just stop and call it quits?" I knew she was baiting the conversation. Once again, she was testing our faith in what we had learned so far. Did we truly believe what she had told us about her family? Was the evidence we had gathered so far nothing more than circumstantial evidence or facts? And yes, I was concerned about the matter. I questioned the things Mr. Evening had said about the dark powers we had to face and the fall out after dealing with evil spirits. But those questions would be held in check. Now was not the time.

The phone was on loudspeaker; Mom and Kendral were listening to the conversation intently. I felt in my spirit Sister had already come to the conclusion that going to Haiti was the only choice she had; and she wanted to know if we would be true to our calling and help her find her family. She simply wanted to hear it come out of our mouths. "Sister" I said slowly, "We believe that from what we have heard, there is a high probability that the woman that raised you is not your mother." Kendral and Momma nodded slowly. I could tell they were like me, hoping I could diffuse Sister and come to a calm place. I continued as cautiously as I could, "I guess…I mean, no not guess but I, I mean we believe (I looked to Kendral and Momma for nods. Kendral had a scathing look and raised his neck, looking like I had said an embarrassing thing. He nodded. Momma just shrugged her shoulders acknowledging that she was onboard if I was. I continued, "Going to Haiti is the only option we have now. Is that what you want to do?" After asking her this question, I could since that had not come out reassuringly to her at all. Though I could not see her, I could imagine her eyes closing and her eyelids twitching as she tried to hold back an outburst of anger. In a gentle, barely controlled voice, she said. "Listen, if you guys are ready to quit, then just say so. I know how you all are feeling right now. It was all fun until it wasn't. I had no idea that things would get so bazaar." I could tell by her voice that her eyes were getting a little wet. She continued, "This is my road, a road I must take to save me from insanity. This road will redeem me of my children and husband, who have continually considered me a fruit basket for most of my life. I have spent countless hours on my knees and shed many tears asking God to guide me to the truth. Now because the road has turned bumpy, I should quit? If I quit now, after all the pain and anguish, what would that say to God?" Gaining more control of herself, she said "No, I choose to go forward. I choose not to be afraid of the very thing that has kept me in bondage, and I choose to be strong in the Spirit of the Lord and not to be ruled by the spirit of fear."

Silence came over us all for a moment. We could hear Sister in the background. Evidently, she had gone to the kitchen and was getting a glass of water from the sink. She leisurely took a few sips from the glass as we said nothing. With her mood seeming to calm down even more, she said, "The unbelief that my family had of what God was showing me caused me great distress. I asked Him to reveal to me the truth and finally He has. I asked Him to help me financially when the time came, and He has. I told Him I was alone and wanted true friends that would believe in Him; and after going through years of potential friends, He chose you. I believe that you were predestined to be here. No one could have taken on this mission if they hadn't had the time to do it. How many jobs would have given you the time off we've needed so far? What about the financing of the whole thing? My money didn't come five years ago, nor did it come five years in the future. It came exactly when God wanted it, right around the time He brought you guys on board. Seriously, all of this was planned by a greater authority. Let's look at some other facts. First, your kids are grown as are mine. Secondly, Brother Kendral, God blessed you to in you in your own business now. You can take off whenever and how long you want. Thirdly, Sister Kathy, you are a home keeper and have all the time to do whatever you need to whenever you want to. Ceil, you are retired and on no one's time clock. I am retired and can do as I will. You cannot tell me that you do not see God's planning here!"

Again silence. I looked around at Mom and Kendral. If shame had a face, we'd be copies of that face. With our heads hung low all I could say was, "You're right." Speaking for the group, I told her that we should move on. And I told her we had gotten a little shaken after Mr. Evening's visit. Then Sister said, "I have absolutely nothing to lose here. As far as I am concerned, my family has privately disowned me. But I do understand how you feel. You guys have something to come back to. I live in an empty house. My husband is dead, and my children are either in another country serving the government, off at college, or just simply can't find the time to share with their mother. So, let's do it this way. When we get to where we are going, I don't want you to go with me to meet Ethell. Once we locate her home, hut, cave or whatever her living situation is, I want you all to stay at the motel and wait for me there. How's that?" I slowly turned to see the expressions on the group's faces. What I saw was shamefulness, so I turned back to the phone and said, "Oh no, we are in with you, all the way. Whatever it takes to find your family, we are in it with you."

Silence hung in the air and through the loudspeaker on the phone we could hear Sister sniffling with tears again. Kendral reached for the phone and he told Sister, "I don't care where we go as long as that old warlock Mr. Evening doesn't go!" Sister, through a giggle said, "Now, Brother, he never said he was a warlock. Be nice. Brother let me ask you something. When you first met me or even now, do you find some things about me weird or just not adding up?" Kendral hesitated, feeling the need to cautiously swirl around the question; but with summed up courage he replied, "Yes, of course. I am sure we all can be weird in our own ways at times. Why do you ask?" She responded, "Yet, am I not a friend? Though my actions may be weird at times, have those actions been distrusting or harmful to you in any way?" Of course, the answer was no. She continued, "Mr. Evening is a very strange fellow indeed, but I believe his intentions are good and honorable. I have a strong feeling that Mr. Evening's presence will be appreciated when we most need it going forward." Without saying a word to Sister, he handed the phone back to me for he knew what Sister had said was true. I took the phone back and asked Sister when she expected to leave for Haiti. She said she had to make a few more arrangements pertaining to hotels in Haiti and question the tour agencies about the best places to find "extracurricular activities" of a certain sort. Sister gathered herself and said, "Let me apologize for being frustrated earlier. You guys have no idea what it would mean to me to connect with my real family, my real mother. I could not have come this far without you guys helping me and keeping me centered. I also believe that there is more here for you guys." Momma asked, "What do you mean?" Sister said, "I don't know, I just feel in my spirit that we will all be rejoicing; not just me, but you guys too when all this is settled." We looked around at each other and grinned. Then we told her we loved her and hung up.

Chapter 9

*I*t was sometime in the middle of June 2008. Sister called us and she had decided by way of the Spirit that in one week we would leave and sail to Haiti. One week later, we drove from our little town of Walterboro, South Carolina to Jacksonville, Florida and began to board the cruise ship. We had decided that this was the cheapest way and that the extra time to travel on a boat compared to speeding to Haiti on a plane would give us time to tie up any loose ends. The plan was simple. We would take the boat to Haiti and get rooms that Sister had already reserved for us. With any luck, we would find Ethell Gush, question her and catch the next flight back to the Americas. Concerning supplies, we packed two weeks' worth of everything. Kendral had mentioned that having at least two weeks' worth of stuff like clothes, band aids, toothpaste, socks, plenty of bottled water, etc., would be a safe bet whenever going to a third world or second world country. I couldn't believe we were going to Haiti. I was grinning the whole time and fantasizing about how beautiful Haiti would be. I had to keep reminding myself this wasn't actually a vacation, and I should act as such. Keep your eyes on the prize, I told myself.

It was my first cruise, and I loved the experience. Several days later, we docked at Port Labadee, Haiti. We had decided to rent a car, which turned out to be an old 1980 Toyota minivan. It looked similar to the one you see Scooby Doo and the Gang driving. It was a steaming, muggy 99 degrees. Luckily, the old van had air-conditioning. We made the deposit, and we were off to our motel. Sister had booked a hotel that had high elevation and sat at the foot of a mountain; so, we could look down at the village. The hotel was situated over the village about two miles out and up. Though we were away from the main town, Labadee, this area had small shops and restaurants as well. The map we had was incredibly useful. Without that we would have had to hire a guide just to get to the motel. We found the motel and paid a kid to help us unload. Sister slipped him ten dollars and asked him to watch our room for strangers or anyone snooping around. The little boy grinned and gave Sister a snapping salute and hurried off! Once inside our room, I went out onto the window balcony to look at the view. It was spectacular! Way off in the distance a row of mountains, covered with greenery, painted the sky! The well-kept white sand dirt road sloped and curved as it led its way back to the town. Along the road, Small cafés and tourist shops littered the area. After unpacking we decided to go out, have a look around and meet some people. The people there were very nice. They mostly wanted to know about America and what brought us to Haiti. We did not mention to anyone why we were actually there, fearing that if someone knew the elusive Ethell Gush, they might give her an advance warning that we were there. We could only assume she would get suspicious knowing someone from America was looking for her because of what Mr. Evening had said earlier, "If Sister finds out you are looking for her, she will immediately set her cronies out to spread misleading details to throw you off her trail."

We were sitting outside a restaurant, under a large beach umbrella, sipping coffee. Sister leaned toward us and said, "Remember the dream I shared with you about the woman and the red stone. I dreamed about her again last night. The same exact dream!" she exclaimed. In the dream, as usual, the lady points to the stone on her forehead and says, "So that you will never forget" but in this dream, she points to a mountain as well. We all turned and looked at the mountain curiously, as it was the backdrop of our seating area. Then to snap us out of our inquisitive look at the mountain; suddenly, a lady around my age, with high cheekbones and long braids walked up to us and in a very heavy Hattian tongue, introduced herself as Frieda. This "Frieda" was tall, and her build was a few notches above skinny. Her hair had many small braids, and her complexion was very dark, but as smooth and clear as a newborn baby. After we all introduced ourselves, we invited her to sit with us and she accepted. We got into a casual conversation and after a few laughs and big smiles, Frieda asked us if we needed a guide. We had been on the Island for about six hours and to be honest, we were getting nowhere fast. I guess Kendral had surmised the conversation needed to turn; so being the instigator that he could be at times, he made the first move. He leaned across the table and looked at our new friend, and asked, "So, this is the land of magic and voodoo huh? Tell me, Frieda, are any of those stories true? I mean really, who believes in voodoo? We all know it's all just a bunch of children's tales." I realized he was baiting her. Sister also realized what he was up to and played along and looked at him with stern eyes and joined in and said, "Brother! Just because our God is real, and voodoo is just babbling words doesn't mean you can insult the natives! You should apologize for that." Then Sister reached out and touched Frieda on the hand and said, "Pay him no mind. Every culture has its myths and legends." Raising her eyebrows, the woman said, "Myths and legends? No need for an apology. Many of "you people" come here with unbelief." I was squirming in my seat, feeling very uncomfortable. Antagonizing is not one of my strong points, so I took another sip of coffee, peeped from the rim of my cup and watched as my cunning husband and sneaky compadre worked on Frieda. Momma was nudging my knee under the table letting me know she, too, had caught on to the game. Sister said, "Enough talk about foolishness and old wise tales, let's talk about real power from on high." Kendral openly shrugged Sister off, pushed on, and came back with, "You know "Frieda" (making quotation marks with his fingers to insinuate his disbelief that her name was ever Frieda), I would pay a pretty penny to see some real black magic at work. Of course, to see the real magic, I would most undoubtedly have to go to the motherland, Africa. All you're going to find here in Haiti is some cheap parlor tricks. Anyone can pull a rabbit out of a hat!" Then he reared back in the chair and laughed so hard he had to hold his stomach. All of that was part of the act too. Frieda had enough of the insults. Without saying a word, she took her gaze off of Kendral, took a sip from her tea, stood and said to the group, "Your attempt to insult my culture has failed. I am not insulted. I will gladly take your "pretty penny" (she mocked Kendral while using her fingers to make quotation marks insinuating, she knew he was mocking her earlier) to show you that black magic is alive and well in Haiti." Kendral, still in character, ending his laughing replied, "I tell you what Frieda, I'll bring the hat if you'll bring the rabbit" and shook his head as if definitely unbelieving. Frieda's eyes became like slits and said, "Meet me back here at 12:45 tonight and bring that pretty penny with you. I will see if I can change your mind about Haiti and its gods!"

With that she turned and walked away. We watched her as she

mingled in and out of the crowd until she disappeared into a building. Sister was smiling at Kendral like she had just figured out the winning lottery numbers and Kendral was looking back at her with a grin that looked like he had just swindled someone out of a car. Me, I was wondering just how much crap we had just plunged ourselves into. Momma, talking to no one in particular said, "I think we might have crossed the line somewhere in that, don't you?" I was nodding my head in agreement. Kendral said in a concerned voice, "We meant no harm to her. We are going to have to be willing to use tactics to get the information we need. I agree it was a strong tactic, but we got to the door"... (Sister cut in and said) ... "And tonight, we are going to walk into that door boldly and I can tell you why... (quoting from the Bible she continued) "Because the Kingdom suffered violence and the violent take it by force!" Sister was so sure of herself and when she was like that, there was no need for debate. For the first time, I actually saw Kendral and Sister in full agreement. To be honest, that was a good thing and reassuring. It had gotten late, around 8:30pm. We decided to go back to the motel to rest a while.

When we got back to the motel, Sister found the little boy who she called Hauchi. They had a conversation as we went on into the room. A few minutes later, Sister came in looking curious and concerned. She said, "We've had a visitor." We turned to look at her and she said, "Hauchi said two men came here looking for us. Hauchi said the man gave him a five dollar so he showed him our room. The man did not request to go in but placed his hand upon the door and said some words the boy did not understand." Kendral asked, "Root work?" Sister shrugged her shoulders, shaking her head unknowingly. She said we should pray about that and also pray for our protection while on this island. So, we did. We had an awesome time in the Lord and out of the haziness of the realm of Glory invoked by praise and worship, we all got the same message, "No weapon formed against us shall prosper!"

Exhausted, we slumped to the couch and chairs. After a short nap, we were refreshed. It was around 12:00 am and our time to meet Frieda was slowly coming up. Kendral decided to go downstairs to look around and see if he could see or pick up on any foolishness going on. I went to the balcony to look from up high to see if I could detect anything as well. We suspected there might be more at play here than just Frieda because of the earlier strangers that visited our room. We decided to take just enough cash for bribes and enough to satisfy the would-be robbers. At 12:30 am we began to walk back to the cafe. The streets were well lit, and we approached as a group, walking and acting confident. We took seats and it wasn't long before Frieda showed up. "You got my pretty penny?" she asked. Kendral took out a twenty-dollar bill and waved it in the air. She said, "I will need it's twin as well." So, looking annoyed, he grabbed another twenty and before giving it to her, he asked, "So what's in store for us tonight, Frieda? Will you stay with us the entire time or leave us in an unfamiliar area with no guide?" She looked at him with a sardonic look and said, "I'm not like you. I'm a decent and honorable person who doesn't go around insulting people and their ways. My upbringing and your money secure your safety. I will not leave you." With that, she rolled her eyes at him and then motioned for us to follow her. We ended up walking about a block where the street lighting got dimmer. You have to understand how this part of Haiti looked…the jungle was not far away from the streets at all. Once you walked off the well beaten paths, the jungle seemed to be always trying to take back its lands. I was nervous so I was constantly looking around. Suddenly, I noticed a figure of a person ahead of us standing under a streetlamp. It was a man who seemed to be waiting, for something. We stopped a few feet away from this shadowy individual, as Frieda approached him alone. She handed him some money and he pointed to a little house. The house set right outside of the influence of the streetlamp; if it had not been for the moon light, we would have missed the house all together! The moonlight casting shadows off of the house, as there were no lights in the house, the placed looked dreadful. Momma said, "I know we're not going into that!" Frieda reassured her that we weren't actually going into the house and that the house was just a front to where we were actually going. We began to walk again, and Frieda led us to the back of the house. At the back, we came upon a two-door cellar that led beneath the house. The two doors were open, and the inside was very dimly lit. Frieda looked around at us all and motioned for us to follow her, so we cautiously did. I was sure from the horror movies I had seen that the doors behind us would slam shut on their own and would lock us in. From that point all hell would break loose. I giggled to myself. I was comforted to know the doors never closed. Kendral kept his hand in mine the whole time while I held on to Momma's. We rounded a wall and entered a small room. Honestly, the scene wasn't too dramatic. The room was filled with different kinds of incense burning away. Kendral gently elbowed me in my side and whispered in my ear, "I think one of those incenses may be some of the local wacky weed." I giggled to myself again. The hue was thick, but the smells weren't toxic to the point where they made you cough. At the center of the room was a large stick pointing out of the ground. Rags had been wrapped around the top of it and the wrapped rags had been set on fire, forming a torch. Next to the stick sat a young boy about eight years old and all he had on for clothing was his underwear. We did not sit because there were no seats. A person wearing a hood approached from another room and stood by the boy. He slid his hood off, and a long, large swath of dry gray dreads fell down over his shoulder down to his waist. The only clothing the man had on was what looked like a large white cloth diaper and a pair of sandals, and that was it! He looked our way and gave a very toothy grin, with a couple gold and brown teeth. He began to chant over the boy and then stopped abruptly. With his foot, he pushed a coffee can toward us. In it were several denominations of American dollars. I could hear Kendral sighing as he reached in his pocket and put two 20-dollar bills in the can. With that, the man began to chant again, and the boy began to have what looked like an epileptic fit. The man continued to chant and then suddenly the boy fell over flat on his back. The boy didn't move. For a few seconds, nothing in the cellar moved. It was so quiet; I could hear my breathing and my heart beating in my chest! The boy had not stirred since he had fallen! Was he dead? My heart began to race, "Are we now accessories to a murder?"

Then the man motioned for each of us to come over and listen for a heartbeat. After Sister raised her head from the boy's chest, she then looked at us calmly and said, "There is no heartbeat, and the boy is not breathing." I am always impressed when Sister did that...In the midst of horror, she somehow finds calmness. Well, I most certainly was not calm. In my head, my thoughts were screaming... "Oh my God! There was no heartbeat! No breathing and the body was lifeless and we were going to rot in a prison!" Kendral, as nervous as he was, leaned toward me and whispered, "Trust the trick." I calmed myself, and as he motioned for me to continue watching. As we sat there waiting for the catch, for the man to bring the boy back, the man began to talk to us in high accented Haitian mixed with English. He asked, "Why are you seeking dark magic?" We glanced at him and then back to the boy. Since the boy had fallen over lifeless, three minutes had passed by. I knew that after eight minutes; the brain would begin to die. I really wanted this guy to fix this boy on the ground!" Sister spoke up and said, "It's not dark magic we are looking for. We are looking for someone." As if not hearing Sister, and noticing our concern for the boy's lifeless body, the man turned his attention to the boy, shook his head and said sadly, "The boy is not dead, he is just not here."

Six minutes had passed by. "His life is suspended." Waving his hands around in the air he continued, "He is watching us from the other realm as we speak." Momma spoke up, "That's all and well and good, but you can bring him back to this realm of course." The man asked in astonishment, "Bring him back? The deal was that you wanted to see black magic and you have. You see lying before you a child who had life; but the body is lifeless. By the Island's magic, he lives on in another realm. That is magic, dark magic! His family sacrificed him for a debt that was owed to me. I took him on as a servant but the money you have paid, (he looked into the jar) will be worth more than what two of him would have been worth." "Are you telling me for twenty-five dollars, you have killed this boy?" Kendral asked explosively, "What, in God's name, is so magical about killing someone? Unless you can bring this boy back to life there is no magic here, only murder!"

By this time, eight minutes had passed by. The man looked confused and said, "Do not worry. Here the laws are different. Paying for someone to be killed here is an everyday thing. No one will ever know you paid for his death and if they did, all I have to do is pitch out a few coins and all is forgotten." Kendral, getting very annoyed, said, "Sir we never asked you to kill anyone, and we certainly believe this boy's life is worth more than twenty-five dollars! And I say again, this is not magic, this is murder! Are you trying to get more money out of us? If so, it's not going to work!" Kendral then looked at Frieda and said, "Well aren't you going to say something!" Ten minutes had passed by now. Frieda, looking just as shocked as we were, finally confronted the man saying, "I assured these people that this would be a safe experience and you, sir, have made it into a fiasco!" Then, she turned to us and said, "We'd better get out of here before someone sees us here and try to pin this

67

on us." Grinning, the man asked, "But who are you seeking? You said you were seeking someone. While the boy is in this other realm, he sees all things. He is omnipresent. Whom do you seek? I will ask the boy. If this person is here on the Island, he will know." Upon hearing this, we all stopped walking out and looked at each other and considered. Without saying a word to us, Sister walked back into the room; holding back tension in her voice and said, "Ask the boy about a woman named Ethell Gush." The man's head slanted to one side. He seemed to consider her request for a moment. (Twelve whole minutes had passed by since the boy fell dead.) Again, with his foot, he slid the coffee can toward her and said, "The cans spirit needs to be 'invoked.' If the cans spirit is invoked enough, then the person you seek shall be found." (Of course, he wanted more money.)

In a commanding voice, with eyes that looked like burning coals in the dim light, Sister pointed her Moses cane at the man and said, "Be warned, demon and hear me well!!" Somewhere deep inside of us the Holy Spirit compelled us to move toward Sister. We grabbed one another's hands and formed a circle around her. With our eyes closed, we fell to the floor on our knees! Sister stood tall in the center of the circle and said, "I have had enough of your pilfering. I will not invoke that can! I want to know where Ethell Gush is and not that she is on the Island, we already know that! And when the boy finds the location, I want you to revive him to his fullness, do you understand? (That wasn't a question! That was a threat, and we all knew it. Sister was beyond being nice.) She continued. "If you don't, so help me by The One True God, we will invoke a spirit as well in this place and His name is The Holy Spirit!" The man seemed to get nervous and held out both hands haltingly said with a trembling voice, "Wait! Wait!" You never told me you were disciples of Yahshua." By this time fifteen minutes had passed since the boy had ceased to live. He still lay on the floor motionless and lifeless. Sister lifted her cane to the air and lit into the man with fervent disdain. "You are a taker of life. A selfish, vile, ungodly creature! You bleed the weak and suffer not. But tonight, it all ends!" Sister went into a tirade, saying. "I decree and declare right here, right before The One and Only, Living God, for the spilled blood on Calvary" ......We began to praise and worship God around her. The air around us felt like small currents of electricity were flowing into us. We swayed back and forth below Sister with chants of indiscernible words. Small dust devils began to form from the dirt floor as Sister continued to raise her cane even higher. The man became very nervous. Putting his hands to his ears, he said, "No, No, No. My time is not yet!" He began to chant over the boy. The boy began to stir and coughed like a resuscitated drowning person.

On seeing this, Sister stopped her decree and we stopped praising as well. The boy slowly sat up. He pointed to the wall as if he was seeing through the wall to another place and said, "Follow the path that leads to Oswake Bridge. Where the path ends, she will come." He repeated, "She will come." Then the boy folded his legs under him, bowed his chin to his chest, closed his eyes and went silent. The man said nervously, "Yes, follow the path to the end and there she will seek you. As you can see the boy is no longer dead. He lives! I ask you, Children of Jeshua, will you leave me in peace, I pray thee?" Sister looked at him and said, "Peace you will never have. You have bonded with your craft, and you do not wish to be free, so we leave you as you were!" The man began bowing as if he all of a sudden had become a Chinese. Frieda had chosen to hide behind us the whole time and was relieved when we motioned for her to lead us out of the house cellar. As we walked back to the motel, no one said a word. We were all in warrior mode. I dared any spirit at that moment to show its ugly face and I knew the rest of the group felt the same way. On the way back to the motel people avoided looking at us. God had set up a hedge around us; we and He have had enough of the foolishness! As we were relieving Freida, she turned back toward Sister and asked, "Was that the Holy Spirit I have heard so much of?" Sister looked at her and quoted from the bible, "Where the lightning strikes, so shall He be." Frieda seemed to understand, as she continued to apologize for the night. Kendral saw her back to the street and returned to find us all trying to unravel. He hugged me and asked if everyone was all right. We all nodded, but you could tell we were all shaken by the ordeal. He tried to make light of it all and tried to ease our minds. He made jokes about who was the most afraid and wanted to run and asked, "why was the witch doctor wearing a diaper." It was a good thing he was there to lighten the mood. Sister joined in as well, but we all knew that this was just the beginning of a shallow hole getting deeper and deeper. After tonight our opportunity at trying to keep Ethell Gush in the dark about someone looking for her would be out. Knowing that, the silent hunt became more of a noisy chase. If only we could locate her before she could gather who was looking for her. If she knew it was Sister, from America, I am sure she would realize something was amiss, especially if she had anything to do with Sister's childhood. The question was, when we finally did meet her, would she embrace us or repel us? Honestly, we had no idea what would happen and that led to much anxiety. Ethell probably would try to find out what we wanted from the voodoo priest, but we left him with as little information as possible. All in all, the excursion was fruitful though, and that was a plus. We were exhausted, so we prayed and went to sleep.

I awoke the next morning around 10:00. I was headed to the breakfast bar; Sister was just leaving her room as well. I was holding the elevator for her as I watched her hand Hauchi a few dollars. On our way down we made small talk and it seemed she and I were the last to the breakfast bar. Momma and Kendral were already halfway through a cup of coffee. We joined them and they respectfully let Sister and I enjoy a few sips of coffee before engaging us in conversation. Kendral leaned back over his chair with both arms out stretching for the ceiling and asked no one in particular, "Ok, what's the plan for today?" Sister eased her cup from her lips just far enough away to move her lips to speak and said, "I have sent Hauchi to find Frieda. We are to meet her within the hour at the coffee shop. I am going to see if she can help us get to this 'Oswake bridge'."

We had a light breakfast of bagels topped with cheese and pineapple slices. After breakfast, we went back to our rooms to gather our backpacks and supplies for the day's venture. We left the motel and waited for Frieda at the coffee shop. It wasn't long before we saw Frieda heading our way. She didn't come directly to us. She mingled in and out of groups of people, stopping here and there to smell flowers or chat with someone she knew. I watched curiously and nudged Kendral's elbow. He nodded to me, never taking his eyes off Frieda. I assume the ever so clever leader of our bunch had told Hauchi to tell Frieda to be discreet when she left her home, as someone might be watching her. She finally made it to our table. Kendral stood and slid a chair out for her near Sister. With this kind gestor from Kendral, I think it dawned on Frieda that we trusted her and any rudeness from him earlier was all a game, intended to get the right information we needed. I could see she was pleased with that. She sat and ordered herself a coffee. Momma, disliking the quietness, smiled at Frieda warmly and asked, "Did you sleep well last night or did the boogie man get at you?" Her coffee arrived. She smiled back at Momma and we gave her nice smiles. Sister never looked up from the table or her coffee. Momma and Frieda carried on a casual conversation for nearly five minutes about the weather, her teaching career, her younger days, etc. As Momma talked, Kendral and I were enjoying a husband and wife's conversation, which caused me to blush. Then, like rising from out of a slow coma, Sister said, "Sister Kathy, isn't there something that we need for Frieda to do for us? It's getting late and I wish to be back here before dark". I was caught completely off guard by this, and my flirting husband sat up in his chair, coming to attention. Evidently, I had been chosen by Sister to mediate this part of the venture or at least open the dialog. I gathered myself and took another sip of coffee, as everyone was looking at me. I looked at Frieda, who by this time was questioning the real intent of being invited to breakfast. I asked, "Frieda can you take us to Oswake Bridge?" Frieda put her coffee on the table and sarcastically said, "And here I thought I had been called for a cup of coffee among my new friends…. The answer to your question, pretty lady, is maybe." When had I become, "pretty lady?" I thought to myself. Shrugging off the thoughts, I asked, "Maybe?" Frieda said, "Finding Oswake Bridge, I can do…if you will tell me what you're up to. You misled me last night. You told me you wanted to see Black Magic; but what you really were looking for is a person. Why did you lie to me? Why not just ask me about Ethell Gush? Why the fiasco? What can Ethell Gush tell you that the witch doctor couldn't tell us last night?" "Well, do you know Ethell Gush?" I asked. She replied, "No I do not, but I could have asked around for you." What she didn't understand was that is exactly what we did not need, someone running around the Island spreading the idea that Ethell Gush was being sought after by some Americans.

For a moment we stared at her, really wanting to let her in on the whole thing. Then Momma, looking at Sister, but talking to Frieda asked, "Do you dream?" Frieda looked at her curiously and replied with a nod. Momma continued, "Have you ever had a dream that was so real or a dream that revealed a hidden truth that you just had to follow up?" Frieda began to lose herself in deep thought as she nodded her head and replied, "But…it was only a dream, so I never took it seriously." Momma, now looking at Frieda, said, "But you see Frieda,

72

one of us has had a dream and the four of us have joined together to see it through." Sister sat quiet as a mouse, seeming well pleased at how well Momma had handled Frieda. "Will you help us?" "Yes, but I am still confused. You are following a dream. I get that, but to what? Why so much secrecy? You can't expect me to be running around here with strangers and not know what I'm getting myself into. You said you just wanted to see Black Magic; but really you were looking for a woman. So, you deceived me from the start. If you could do that then, why should I go running off with strangers?" Frieda explained, looking a little hurt. She had a point. Momma took a deep breath, turned to look back at Sister, leaned back in her chair and said, "That is not my story to tell." Kendral, Momma, Frieda, and I turned to look at Sister. Sister, still looking into her coffee, said, "Ethell Gush has information that I need to find my real family." "How did you lose a family?" Frieda asked, looking around the table quite confused. "No. I have never met my real family," Sister replied. Looking as if she had figured it out, Frieda said, "Oh you were adopted, and you are seeking your true family then?" Sister now looked up directly into Frieda's eyes and said, "There is no adoption agency that has my records on file. All written information I have found has suggested that the life I lived was a normal one." Sister hesitated a few seconds, looking saddened, and took a long sigh. I placed my hand gently on her shoulder to comfort her. She smiled at me warmly, placed her hand on mine, and with strength returning, she continued. "All I know is that the person who raised me is not my real mother. I have ruled out adoption. If I were adopted, where is the paper trail? At 65 years old, don't you think someone in my family, surely by now would be willing to tell me the truth? Adopted, one could say that; but if it was done, why has it been hidden from me for most of my life. I have never seen or heard of such craziness! At some point all adoptees learn the truth. That leads me to believe that only one or two people know the truth and are trying to take it to their graves, or everyone is in on it. But the latter I have ruled out as well. We all know the more people know of secrets, the less of a chance it will stay a secret. So, I have settled for the former. I have challenged those in my family, who are old enough to have answers, and all of them except one, has unknowingly given me a clue. And because of that clue, the dream has become more relevant." She hesitated, but this time she was looking like the warrior we knew she could be and with her confidence renewed, she spoke boldly. "I have always felt like a stranger among the family that raised me." Frieda, looking wide eyed as a child looking at her first baby doll, held up a finger stopping Sister, "What was the dream?" Sister said, "I began having the dream when I was only twelve years old. It became a recurring dream, a dream that plagued me and comforted me at the same time. The dream was of an unknown lady with a red stone on her forehead. She would point at the stone and would say to me, "So that you will never forget…find Ethell Gush" and then the dream would end." Frieda honestly looked like she believed Sister, as if she had told her a fact and not a dream. Frieda said, "Here on the Island, dreams rule us. We are guided by them and we honor the Dreamers. Well, I don't know what other clues led you to Haiti, but I believe your dream was the starting point. I, too, am curious about where it might lead."

She looked at her watch and continued, "Yes I will help you at your expense, of course." We all nodded in agreement. Kendral stood to his feet and suggested we should be on our way. We had driven the van down in anticipation of having to travel today. The further we drove from the village, the rougher and narrower the road became. It was so surreal. Natives were walking along the roads and it reminded me of watching African documentaries from the Discovery Channel. The landscape was jungled and mountainous. In the back of the van, we struggled for comfort as the van_dipped and lunged on the rough road. Sometimes the road narrowed to one lane and we could look out the window and look straight down into deep mountain ravines. After about forty-five minutes, the road suddenly flattened out. We left a mountainous area and entered a valley. This was all agricultural farmlands. Wheat, banana trees, and corn seem to go for miles. Every now and then you could see a person waving to us from the fields as we passed by. Then the van came to a stop at the other side of the valley, where the edge of the farmland ended. Frieda stopped at a road shack and began to talk to a woman selling vegetables. When she came back, she said, "The lady said that the road to the bridge is washed out and is impassable by car. We can walk though. The bridge is only a mile down the road. Are you guys good with that?" Sister spoke up for the group with a simple, "Of course". We parked the van, got out our small backpacks and began to walk down the road toward what I hoped would soon bring this trek to a good end. The road soon began to look more like a wide path instead of a road, with high green grasses growing all over it. I questioned speaking to nobody in particular, "Why would anyone choose to live back here?" Momma said, "Every root worker I have ever known worked in secrecy. It is the way of the wicked". We were walking single file with Frieda leading, then Sister, Momma, me, then Kendral. We finally came to an opening and true enough, at the top of a small hill, we began to see what was left of an old bridge. A large wooden panel hung across the bridge that said, QSWAKE Bridge.

Chapter 10

THE WICKED

E thell Gush awoke that morning feeling sluggish; but after a cup
of hot tea, she began to feel a little better. She decided to walk the
perimeter of her knee-high grassed yard that morning while the dew
was still thick. She went over to her goat pen. Her old milk goat was
soundly asleep, and the chickens were still roosting above the goat on
their nests. The sky was blue with only four small white clouds. As she
peered up into the sky, she took a deep breath and exhaled slowly as if
to taste the early morning air. As with any other morning, it was very
quiet. Ethell enjoyed this time of the morning, right before the sun rose.
The birds were not whistling, frogs had stopped calling and crickets had
stopped chirping. Usually, the only sounds Ethell would hear would be
the sound of her own breathing and footsteps on the ground, but this
morning would be different.

Breaking her mild nostalgia, hearing an uncommon early morning
sound, she knew this was very unusual for this time of morning. "Hoot!
Hoot! Hoot! Hoot!" It was the sound of an owl. Being the person

that she was, she was highly in tune with things most people never noticed. Hearing the sound of the owl hooting four times, brought her to attention. She said to herself, "Wait a minute girl, that's the second set of fours." Thinking back, she also realized that the sky was clear and only four small white puffy clouds were present. As long as I have lived, I have never heard an owl do more than three calls in a cadence! The powers that be are trying to tell me something." She made her way back to her house. As her foot touched the first of the four steps leading up to her porch, she saw movement out of the corner of her eye. Four doves landed in her little garden and headed toward her house. As they walked, the doves called four times repeatedly until they reached the house. Then they flew away. Being convinced something was afoot, Ethell continued to the inside of her shack. She knew what had to be done to confirm her belief about the signs she had gotten. She took her teacup and poured water into it. Then she took two matchsticks and broke them in half. She gave the water one complete stir, cast in the broken matchsticks and commanded over the cup, "I can see you, but you can't see me. You have a secret. Tell it to me!" She knew if the sticks lined up horizontally, nothing was amiss; but if they lined up vertically, there was an issue. The sticks lined up vertically and not only that; they were stuck together, no space between them! Ethell stared at the now motionless cup and thought to herself, "So I am having company, four to be exact. They are of one mind but when should I expect them?" At that moment, a crow landed on her windowpane and began to crow while looking toward Oswake Bridge. It flew off, found a tree and continued to crow towards the bridge. Ethell quickly stood; grabbed her walking cane and began to walk toward Oswake Bridge. The bridge was just beyond a patch of old grown oak trees, about a five-minutes' walk. Once she got within shouting distance of the bridge, she eased off of the path and stood among the trees, out of direct sight. She waited and wondered if these visitors were friend or foe. She mused, "If the strangers were bringing trouble, they would be the ones that would need help, not me!" She grinned at the idea of unleashing a spell or two on an enemy. Soon she saw something floating in the water, coming down the river. She eased out into the open to get a better look at the floating object. It was some broken planks that had come together to form a cross. As it floated by, Ethell stared at it and then she looked up to the inside of the bridge. On one of the old rusty metal beams, someone had sprayed a cross. "Ahhh…It's Yahshua's disciple's that come to visit. This should be interesting!" she said to herself, now more curious than ever. "No matter. I have dealt with these kinds before, and they are no different than the rest of His 'beloved'. They come wearing their Godly inheritance like a coat, as if they are special; but after a few minutes of talking to them, I have found greed with no personal sacrifice and cowardness rules them like it rules the rest of us. Rarely have I found any of them that are true believers. They are His children in name only. I will disseminate them as one cuts up chicken!" She reassured herself with that thought and with a sneaky grin, eased back into the edge of the woods.

It wasn't long before Ethell began hearing chatter coming in the direction of the bridge. Ethell decided to reveal herself instead of hiding. "I need not show fear here. I need to show full confidence," she thought. "Why should I hide?" So, she stepped out from the woods right up to the edge of the bridge. She wanted to be in full view and give the impression that she was expecting them, for she was. She thought, "This should give them the idea that any plans of catching me off guard, will be fruitless."

As our group of five continued to walk, the bridge came into full view. We noticed an old lady standing on the other side of the bridge. She seemed harmless, so we focused more on the bridge than her at the moment. The bridge was old and made of metal and wood. Walking across it wouldn't be a challenge; but this bridge's time of being able to handle vehicle traffic had long gone! I noticed Frieda's head turned to the direction of the old lady. Our heads followed. The old lady's clothes looked ragged and old. She was dressed like she could have walked out of a slave field from the movie Roots. She had a cane, which looked similar to Sister's; but from hers hung small animal skulls. She also had a homemade corn cob smoking pipe hanging loosely from her mouth. Remembering what the young boy had said that night about Ethell, I asked, "Is that her?" No one said anything. Frieda led us closer to the bridge. Right before we stepped on the bridge, Frieda yelled across the bridge, "We are looking for Ethell Gush!" All of a sudden, you could hear birds rushing to take flight and animals fleeing through the woods. "That was weird," Kendral said. The old lady raised her cane. A soft breeze came over the woods and the animals seemed to settle down. Then she spoke in a very soft voice from her distance of about 50 feet away. We shouldn't have been able to hear her, but her voice seemed to travel on the wind. "I am she and I have been waiting for you." The lady turned and began to walk away from us.

Ethell's words gave me the freaking chills so bad, I felt like running back to the van, but Kendral came up beside me, smiled, and said, "This ought to be fun." "Should we follow?" Frieda asked. Sister turned to us and said, "This is the place where I will ask you not to come. I would like for you all to stay here and to pray for…" I cut her off and said, "Sister, like I said before, we love you and we are for you. Nothing is going to keep us from helping you. Nothing." I took three large steps toward her. Momma followed and said, "In for a penny, in for a pound!" Sister smiled and looked very proudly at us as a tear rolled down her cheek. We turned back to the lady, claiming to be Ethell Gush. She mocked, "You have come this far, but now you quiver? Are you not Yahshua's disciples? "Come seek and you shall find." Isn't that what your Bible teaches?"

At that, Frieda spoke up. "Well, I think I've had my fill of all this. I will go back to town and wait for you there." We hugged her and she headed back to the farm fields. Sister stepped forward to lead, as we followed her as she followed after Ethell. As we walked along the path, the day began to seem to get a little darker the further we walked. Momma whispered, "There is some powerful juju working here." I nodded to her.

As we followed Ethell up the path, we kept a slight distance away from her...or was she keeping a distance from us? It was odd. It was like she knew our intentions were not the usual. Her normal customers would come seeking advice, but she was acting like we were more like a sneaky bunch trying to snare her. "Is that why we were here, to snare her? I asked myself. Why would she be acting distant unless she already knew something was not normal about our visit? Things didn't have to go sour as long as Ethell was courteous and helpful, right? What harm could be caused by simply asking some questions? I also thought about the things Mr. Evening had said about her. "Ethell could be very crafty, if she needed to be." I was just about to stop the four of us and simply ask Sister for answers, when suddenly Sister stopped to tie her shoe. When she stopped, we stopped as well, but Ethell kept walking.

First of all, I noticed her shoes didn't need tying. She pretended to tie her laces, and said, "Let the Holy Spirit lead you." Then she said a quick prayer, "Father, we invoke the Holy Spirit for protection, wisdom and powerful discernment; and may Your will be done." Well, there was my answer. Hell was probably going to break loose, and this is the battle we had trained for. We began to walk again and as we topped another small hill along the road, we entered an opening in the woods. In the center of the plot of land was a small house that was not far from being a shack. Was that a goat on the porch?

The house sat on about a half-acre of land. There was nothing unusual about its appearance, surprisingly. I was expecting old bones hanging from the porch or at least some dream catchers hanging around; but there were none. Ethell stopped and said, "This is my home, and you are all welcome. I will make some tea. Please have a seat wherever you like." We found several chairs on the old shack's porch and positioned the chairs where two of us sat on one end of the porch while the other two sat on the opposite end, to make sure Ethell could only seat herself toward the center of us. We cautiously looked around the yard and peeped in through the screen door as Ethell continued to put a pot on the stove and set several cups on the table. Sister looked over at us and I could read her like a newspaper. "We should be on our toes" was written all over her face. Soon Ethell brought out a tray with a pot of steaming hot water and some cups and placed it on the porch table. She proceeded to pour the hot water over fresh tea leaves that were in every cup.

Then as a good host should, she passed a cup to each of us. We watched her quietly as she dragged another chair from inside the house and sat down, feeling very pleased with herself. As she was sitting, she slapped both her hands on her thighs and asked, "So what brings you lovely folks to this part of the world?" She looked around the group to see who would speak, trying to figure out which of us was in charge. For a slight moment, no one spoke. So, to throw Ethell off, Sister unperceptively nodded to Kendral. "Well, I guess you could say we are here looking for someone but were actually looking for someone for her." Kendral pointed to Sister, who smiled angelically. He took a shallow breath and continued. "She is looking for her mother. We believe that you have information that might lead us to her." By this time, Ethell was looking confused and asked, "You mean, I might be able to locate her, or do you mean I might know who she is? And why am I talking to you, if she is the one searching?" We looked toward Sister. Her head was covered by her hoodie robe. The shade of the trees cast her in a dark glow. She stared at Ethell like a hawk. Her cane rested between her legs and on her shoulder. Her eyes looked like hot coals, but she said nothing. Kendral replied, "To answer your first question, you may have met her mother some years ago, fulfilling the request of a client.

Secondly, she will speak when she feels her voice needs to be heard." All of this wrangling was done to keep Ethell off balance and to let her know she was not in control. Realizing she was not dealing with simpletons, Ethell asked politely, "Ok, whom might this client be?" From the far end of the porch, Sister, seemingly coming out of some kind of deep vision, finally spoke up. Looking directly into Ethell's eyes and using a more direct tone, she said, "His name was Buddy Tolan. I am not sure when you first met him." I noticed she said that as if she already knew Ethell had met him. She gave Ethell no room to lie. "The time I am focusing on is somewhere in the early to mid-40's." I noticed Ethell squirmed a little, but then she regained her composure. Ethell went into her under garment and pulled out a smoking pipe and lit it. Then she calmly said, "You Americans and your democracy are truly captives of your own inventions. Under the disguise of freedom and justice, you deny yourself the real fruits of your labor. Here on the Island, we cannot be ensnared by your laws. Yes, I was paid to do a deed; but that is in the past, and that is where it will stay."

Immediately, we realized Ethell knew exactly what Sister was talking about. And if that was true, it did not take a lot of investigative work for her to figure out who Sister was, in relation to the deed. Feeling completely in charge, she took a few more pulls from her pipe and then let the smoke roll out her nose like a long parade. Well, I thought to myself, "Battle it is then." Sister was already reaching her snapping point, and she came to her feet, realizing that Ethell was not going to play nicely. When I saw her stand so abruptly, I cunningly stepped between Sister and Ethell and said gently, "You know Ethell, you were like a legend in your day." Sister calmly sat back down, not liking my intervention; but trusting that I knew what I was doing. "We heard all kinds of rumors of how strong your juju was back then. Her eyebrows rose when I said, "back then" and the word "juju." "I see you have retired to live out your days reminiscing about the past and being happy with that. Actually, we have already heard the story of how you did what you did at that hospital for Mr. Buddy." I laughed a little and continued, "I don't think that was much juju at all." After glancing at Kendral, he quickly caught on.

Kendral turned to Sister and said, "Sister, you're wasting your time here. These people have no real magic; they just do evil crap. That's nothing new!" I nodded my head to Kendral and picked up from there saying, "They claimed you caused a severe storm that night, using your juju to put out the lights. We know full well a faulty electrical cable at the power plant caused the whole thing and not your juju. Actually, I have been trying to tell Sister this whole time that what you did was a simple trick. The old hag turned to me quickly and shouted with a threatening voice, "Shut up, Shut up! You don't know what you are talking about! You weren't there!" I tell you the truth, her outburst scared the willies out of me, but realizing she had just placed herself at the hospital during the event was well worth the effort. Realizing that very same fact, she calmed herself. I summoned some courage and continued, "No, I wasn't there, but it is obvious that what you did was not the thing everyone claimed it to be. How hard is it to pay off someone to slip into an electrical plant and wreak havoc?" As I spoke Momma nodded her head in agreement. Somewhere deep inside of Ethell, something broke. Her pride in her work would not allow her to just sit there and be insulted. She suddenly rose to her feet, pointed at me, and began to chant unknown words. But like a flash of lightning, Sister's arm came around to the front of me pushing me back behind her as she stepped in-between me and Ethell, pointed her cane at Ethell and began to speak in the unknown tongues as well! They began to circle one another shouting unknown words, Sister spoke in English accusing Ethell of the dirty deeds, while she accused Sister of being a hypocrite and not a true believer. Far off, I could hear thunder rumbling. One accusation after the other, back and forth they went. After many minutes of chanting, she and Sister stopped pointing and chanting and fell quiet. The air around us became heavy. Seemingly by itself, coffee cup slid off the table and splashed to the floor and like trained soldiers, we were on our knees again with our hands raised and speaking the tongue of the angels! Realizing that she was completely outnumbered, and that Sister would not be moved, Ethell shouted, "You fools! I am Ethell Gush! I was a member of the Coven before you knew what light was! I do not need mere pills and teas to seduce men! Yes, I did as your father paid me to do. I took you away from your real mother! It was me who pulled you from your mothers' womb. It was my hands that washed you and cradled you and placed you in the stead of another! It was the right thing to do. Your father did not love your birth mother. Why should she be the happy one, while the woman he actually loved, grieved over her dead child?" Hearing that, I was sickened to the core. This woman had made a decision that only God should have made! deep inside of me I knew a reckoning was coming!

Suddenly from behind us, we heard what sounded like sizzling electricity and from a haze of smoke, stood none other than, Mr. Evening! He slammed the bottom tip of his cane onto the porch floor to bring us to attention. He was alone this time, without his helper. Mr. Evening said, "I think I have heard enough. What you have done

Ethell is inexcusable." She looked at the old man, as if she did not know who he was. "You don't recognize me, do you? Let me make myself clearer to you. He waved his hands in front of himself as if washing a window. Like a veil being slid away, there stood a man (not bent over and aging, but a middle-aged man) looking quite healthy! "Evening!" Ethell blared. Like a deer trying to bolt over a fence, she leaped over the porch railing trying to run for the woods; but Mr. Evening raised his hand and snapped his fingers. When her feet hit the ground, it was like she was frozen in place! Mr. Evening looked at Sister and said, "It is good to see you again dear. If there is something you wish to know from Ethell, now is the time to ask. I fear she won't be on 'this side' for much longer."

Sister walked off the porch and faced Ethell. "Tell me about my mother." Ethell replied, "I will tell you nothing unless I get some reassurance from Evening that my hearing will be before the counsel coven, and not here amongst mere children!" Evening nodded and Ethell began to speak. "Your father was a military man. He was dating a woman while he was married to another. Both women became pregnant about the same time and both gave birth at the same time. One of the ladies was an Indian exchange student at the college and the other a waitress at a restaurant." I thought to myself, "Indian?" As Ethell took a moment to test the binding cast Mr. Evening had put her in, I whispered to Momma and Kendral, "That explains why in the dream the woman had a red stone on her forehead. In India the people commonly use a colored stone on their foreheads to indicate cast or status. It's an old system that helps govern the Indian people. Realizing that the binding spell was solid, Ethell continued. "The problem for Buddy was that he loved the waitress more than he loved the exchange student; so secretly he married the waitress but continued to see the exchange student. He still had a problem though. The exchange student had refused to have an abortion at your father's request. She told your father that he didn't have to be in the child's life, but he would have to pay child support for the child. For your father, this was not going to work; because he did not want his new wife to know that he had been unfaithful. Neither woman ever knew about the other one. Unfortunately, the wife's baby died, and your father was heartbroken. The Indian woman's baby was healthy and strong; but your mother died giving birth." Sister's eyes began to swell with tears and there was no doubt; It had dawned on Sister that the woman in the photo and the woman in her dream was actually her mother reaching out to her from the other side, letting her know who she truly was. Ethell continued, "Your mother's name was Kalana Postrell. You will find her family in the Hilbram District of India."

Sister was stirred so badly that Momma came down from the porch and led her back to the porch to be seated. But for me, something was still missing. I faced Ethell and asked, "Wait a minute! How did Mr. Tolan know one child was going to die and your service would be needed?" Sister stopped halfway back up the steps realizing she had not thought of that. Ethell looked back to Mr. Evening and then with sad eyes and shaking her head said, "Initially I was not paid to switch the children. Mr. Tolan actually hired me to make sure that the woman that he didn't love... well, that her child did not leave the hospital alive. I was not going to physically hurt the child, just make sure the child naturally aborted. But nature dealt her own hand, and we were left to pick up the pieces. So, we put the living with the living and the dead with the dead. At the time, it seemed fitting." Hearing this, I shook my head. Inside I was raging! I couldn't believe it! This woman was actually going to kill an unborn baby and not realize that is the same as killing it after it was born! What evil! I began breathing heavily. My fist balled up and my teeth began to grind. This wasn't warrior mode I was feeling; this was kick butt mode, and I was ready to engage! As I began the process in my mind about where to strike this very evil woman; suddenly, before I raised my fist, a simple thought creeped into my mind. I turned and locked eyes with Sister. And at that very moment, I knew what she knew. Ethell had mentioned murdering a child, and that child was supposed to be…her! Not only that, but Sister was also supposed to end up on a shelf, in a jar, at Halley's Herb's! So, in other words, Sister was looking at the person called to kill her even before she was born, her murderer! That meant that God intervened in Sister's life, even before she was born! God already knew what evils lay before her and all the good she would do as a Christian. She was supposed to die as a child; but what was meant for evil, was turned to good. So that Sister would live and fulfill her Godly mandate, the other child died naturally. I know a lot of people wouldn't see the fairness in this; but it's simple to us, "His will above all wills." Now I understood why Mr. Evening was there. Ethell had not done the deed of murder but was willing to do the deed. She was inexcusable and he was going to make sure she paid for it! I paused for a moment so Kendral asked Mr. Evening a question. "Mr. Evening, how did you know where we were?" Mr. Evening smiled, "I have been with you since you left America." I was on the cruise boat. I too had a room in the same motel as you, and I blessed your room while you were out. Who do you think Frieda talked to that night on the sidewalk? I was not about to let you face this alone." He placed his hand on Ethell's shoulder and led her behind the house. We decided to see where he was going. We were only about ten paces behind them. Ethell and Mr. Evening rounded the corner and as we rounded the same corner of the house, they were gone! "How does he do that?" Kendral asked. I shrugged.

The trip back up the Atlantic coast to Jacksonville, Florida and back to South Carolina was a sobering recollection of the past few days. Even though Sister seemed pleased, she had sadness about her and seemed detached in most of our conversations. I wasn't the only one that noticed her state of mind. After we got home, I called Momma and I asked her what she felt was bothering Sister. Kendral had come in after feeding his dog. He sat down and motioned for me to put the phone on loudspeaker. Momma had said that she believed Sister felt like the person who had the last contact with her Momma would probably never be seen again. Of course, that person was Ethell Gush. Momma said if she had been in Sister's shoes, she would be wondering why her family in India never came looking for her. I wondered about that myself and then Kendral said, "Maybe they didn't know about her pregnancy." But I replied, "Surely Sister's mother must have told someone in her family she was expecting? If Sister has rationalized the subject using this scenario, then now we know why she is feeling empty and incomplete." Momma said, "Let's give her some time, a few days, maybe even a week to think about everything alone. When the time is right, we will call her up and feel her out." "That sounds like a good idea", I said. We let six days pass before we called Sister and requested a prayer service. She agreed and we met on a Friday night around 7:30. The huge dining table, or as Sister had dubbed it the "Prayer Table", could seat eight people. To have plenty of room to dance before the Lord, we had decided earlier on the seating arrangements. Sister always sat at the head of the table in the largest and highest chair; Kendral sat opposite her at the other end; I sat in one of the side chairs, the middle of the three; and Momma sat opposite me on the other side in the middle of three chairs. Once we all sat down, Sister began to speak to us about all the things she had hoped for. Unfortunately, she felt like anything going forward would be unfruitful. She seemed fulfilled at finally knowing the truth and being vindicated but saddened just the same to know that her story had come to an end. Sister paused to wipe tears from her eyes and continued, "My mother is dead, the woman that raised me and who I thought was my mother is dead, and my father is also dead." I replied. "Let's take it to God and see what word we may get on the matter." Sister replied, "Sister Kathy, what good would that do? Obviously, my family cares little for me or they would have come for me long ago. I would be a bastard child to them, an embarrassment. I mean, that is what I am, a bastard child am I not?" Momma and I realized at that moment what had Sister so down. The room became quiet, and it seemed like a light fog came into the room. The lights dimmed and the ceiling fan began to spin ever so slightly. We knew exactly what this was. It was the Holy Spirit among us to comfort and to guide. We closed our eyes and began to pray. Midway into prayer, something strange was happening to Kendral. I had noticed he had not bowed his head nor closed his eyes. Something seemed to be brewing inside of him, and he was looking at Sister like he could reach across the table and strangle her. I looked at him and asked, "Is something wrong?" Then he stood and almost shouting at no one in particular said, "How dare you! Get thee behind me Satan! You are the father of all lies! There is no truth in you, and you have no authority here! In the name of Jesus Christ, I cast you out and by the power of The Most-High God cast you back to the dark hole you come from!" Sister was completely frozen, and Momma and I were shocked. What had come over Kendral? We had never seen him like this. He seemed to be in a daze. Sister dropped her head into her hands and wept. And then with a softer, but stern voice, Kendral pointed to Sister and asked, "By the living God of Abraham, Isaac, and Jacob, who are you?" He repeated, "Who's child, are you? To whom do you belong ?!" Feeling led by an unseen power, Momma and I stood and went over and stood beside Sister, facing Kendral. I felt guided to put my left hand on Sister's right shoulder, and Momma put her right hand on Sister's left shoulder. Feeling supernaturally recharged, Sister looked up at Kendral and said in her commanding voice, "I am child of the God of Israel and I will not be denied my birthright!" At that, Kendral seemed to come out of his daze and slumped back to his chair. We found our way back to our chairs as well, and we rested our heads onto the table, completely exhausted. A few moments passed and Sister said exactly what we thought she would. "We're going to India!" Then like a Commander and Chief, she began dishing out commands." Sister Kathy, if you would, begin to organize flight tickets, best time to travel, etc..... Brother Kendral, please go ahead and prepare a list of all the items you think we will need for this trip and find out as much as you can about this Hilbram District in India. Elder (This is what she often called Momma.), I will need you to be with me as I acquire the funds and be my helpmate. Would you do that?" Momma nodded, and then there was silence. Noticing the silence Sister looked up at us from a calendar she had pulled from a drawer. "What? You guys do want to finish this, right? Don't tell me that after all we've been through and what we know now, you're having doubts?" "Of course not," I said. "We are all on board. I am amazed at how you bounced back so quickly." Sister dropped her hands to her side in a dismissive way and admitted, "Going to India has been my direction since Ethell Gush spilled her beans. I have been concerned about you guys. I thought that you might decide that going to India would be too much for you, and I would have to go alone. I could not do that. I need my friends, my team, to help me and support me. Without you guys, none of this would have happened. I need you." At that we stood, did a group hug, said another prayer to God, and went home to rest.

Later on, I called up Sister with a serious question. How she was going to be able to prove to her Indian family that she was who she said she was. Sister said a DNA test could validate that. I agreed. We would first find her family, present her and go from there. So, for the next month, we prepared. Somewhere in 2008, we had managed to pull everything together. My youngest child was twenty-one and at the University of South Carolina (USC) in Columbia; and the eldest is twenty-five and attending the local trade school. Leaving them to fend for themselves would be tough. I had my Sister would check on them constantly.

It was 2:00 in the morning on a Tuesday in Charlotte, North Carolina. We got on Delta flight 4487, and we were off. Somewhere above the Atlantic, I fell asleep and dreamed I was floating in a lake. The water was calm, and the sky was as blue as turquoise. Rose petals were floating down from the sky into the water all around me like rain.

Chapter 11

INDIA

Before we left the United States, Kendral had done as much research as he could on the Hilbram District. We landed at Kadapa Airport. It was the closest airport to the Hilbram District area. Unlike America, you don't have to flag down cabs; they flag you down! The cab drivers rushed up to us, competing with the other drivers, and one of them ushered us into his cab. After securing our luggage and before we could tell him where we wanted to go, he just pulled off. The whole procedure happened so quickly that we had already traveled a block before he finally looked over the seat to us and asked, "Where would you like to go?" We told him we wished to go to the American Consulate. Once we got there, we would submit the supposed Indian name of Sister's family and see what popped up.

After we arrived at the Consulate's office, we paid our entrance fee, which was actually an illegal charge to us. But if it moved the process along, then Sister was willing to pay. From there, we waited in the waiting room. India was exactly as I had seen on TV. A different culture than America, but similar in some ways. The people were nice; and once they realized we were Americans, they smiled even larger. Eventually, a secretary came out and motioned for us to come back to one of the offices. When we entered the room, we saw a very dark-skinned man sitting behind a desk. He had a small light blue colored dot at the center of his forehead. He wore a deep blue suit and had jet black hair. This was the darkest skin complexion I had ever seen on a human being. Later on, we would find out that this dark skin reflected one of the higher casts in the country. (I smiled as I thought to myself, now there is something you don't see in America) So his cast, preselected the man to hold a high title as, an Administrator. The man motioned for us to sit. He spoke in a highly Indian accented voice as he asked us questions about why we were there and what were our intentions. Unwilling to tell him everything, fearing that he might try to hide some information, we beat around the bush a little. But he was not a stupid man. He threw up his hands, motioning for us to stop talking, and said, "Let me be clear with you. The family name you have so noted is a well-respected family. I am sure that the family would not appreciate someone coming in from another country claiming to be a long lost relative. Especially a relative presumed to have died years ago, only to gain some influence based on treachery. It is my job to distinguish what is applicable and what is not. I cannot do that without some sort of proof. So please, indulge me or this motion will end here and now!" At this, Sister's fair skin turned a little red and we knew that this high and mighty officer was getting ready to get a piece of her humbling love. Sister stood up and began gently and slowly saying, "I have lived a lie for most of my life. A life created and perpetuated by people who never asked me what I wanted. I have served my time with them. They have gotten the best of me and dealt me a blow that I have not taken well." Her tone increased a little. "Now, as you so put it, let me make myself clear! We have dealt with your bribery fees; I have submitted myself to being all but kidnaped by your so-called taxi drivers; and now my intelligence is being insulted! If for some reason, I am who I say I am and this family found out that you tried your best to keep their lost loved one away from them, I will make it my business to make sure that they know what kind of person you are!" The man began to shift in his seat. "Furthermore, I too, have powerful people in America, who know powerful people in India, (of course this was not true, but that's all we had) who can move this process along a little faster. I have not used them; because I was told you were the man who could get things done. If you are not that person, please direct me to the real man who is in charge!" By the time she was finished, she had both hands on his desk and was leaning over towards him, looking him straight in the eyes. His head had beads of sweat running down his forehead, and he was trying fanatically to hide his nervousness. As he panned the room to look at us, we were as straight-faced as solid stone and our eyes said, "We will not be defeated!" Without warning, Sister turned to Kendral and said, "Brother Kendral!" Kendral came to his feet playing his part and coming to attention as if he was a soldier. "Yes ma'am!" he replied. "Please send an email to the Indian Embassy in America to Director and Overseer Anhui's secretary that we are having some difficulties…." In full character, Kendral pulled out his laptop from his bag and opened it. The man behind the desk quickly responded with both hands out, palms facing us, "Wait, Wait! There is no need for difficulty. Let me make a call to the residence and see if the family can receive visitors at this time. But I make you no promise, is that okay?" "That will be fine." Sister replied, leaning back up from the man's desk and moving away from him. While the man was on the phone, I noticed a large map along the wall. I got up and walked over to it. I wanted to give the man the impression that our going home empty handed was not in his best interest nor was it an option. So, while he waited for someone to come on the phone, I asked him, "Where is the Hilbram District located?" He hesitated and looked over to Sister and Kendral. Kendral was typing on the laptop wanting the man to think he was typing to someone of importance; and Sister gave him a cold-eyed stare that made him snap back into submission. The man quickly replied, "It is located at the east of the capital, along the East river." I scrolled down the map with my finger and found the area. "What kind of area is it?" I asked. He said that it was a large farming area allocated by the King of India hundreds of years ago to the Postrells. "Are they well off? We are not accustomed to the caste system here. If they are poor, we do not want to make them feel ashamed." He replied, "Some of them are... (He looked at Sister's skin.), but I don't think your friend is of the upper caste. I suspect her blood line may have come out of the subfamilies that worked the fields." I knew in my heart, Sister wanted to strangle this man. Momma placed her hand on Sister's hand to calm her. After a short conversation on the phone with someone, the man hung up the phone and said, "The lady of the house is leaving the country for an unknown time. As we speak, she is on her way to the airport." Sister stood again, and with high authority asked, "What is her name? What airport and what time does her flight leave?" The man began to back track and stutter as he absolutely did not want to give out this information. More aggressively, Sister repeated her request, "Her name, the airport and the departure time!" The man was caught off guard by this tall, independent woman standing in front of him demanding him to do things. Nervously, he began punching on his computer and quickly replied, "Emelia Postrell, Lugwith Airport, flight 469 to Ghana, 2:30pm." Without a second to lose, we all stood. Sister walked out first, followed by Momma; then Kendral and me. I turned to the man, shrugged and then closed the door, as if to say, "We tried it the easy way; but you played hardball, so you left us no choice but to play hardball too."

We rushed back to the waiting cab and told the cab driver to hurry to the airport. Along the way, we got held up several times by farmers walking sheep or goats to the markets and automobiles getting stuck in mud. When we got there, we asked the attendant at the window about the flight. Unfortunately, we had missed the flight. Saddened, we sat at one of the sidebar shops and ordered hot tea. The sadness led to a slight depression. The café was crowded. Sister excused herself to use the restroom. A very dark-skinned Indian woman walked over to our area and, seeming a little frustrated, asked if she could have a seat. The Indian lady looked to be well in her 80's. We nodded and she took a seat next to Momma. She took a handkerchief from her purse and wiped her forehead and mouth. She ordered tea and took a deep breath and let it out slowly. Then she asked had we missed our flight too. I told her no, we were trying to catch a friend, but had missed her. She said that she was sorry to hear that and told us that the car she was traveling in, had a flat tire. The lady continued saying she was on flight 469 to Ghana and we responded with, "What a coincidence, because that's the same flight our friend was on." By that time Sister was coming out of the bathroom and was headed to the table. When Sister pulled back her chair to be seated, she also pulled back her hoodie and the lady looked up at her and seemed to lose all color, as if she had seen a ghost! Her eyes locked on Sister. She began to make a strange noise in her throat; almost as if she was trying to speak but could not. We did not know what to do. The woman said in a low voice, "My God, you look exactly like my sister." Momma, Kendral, and I slowly looked at Sister and then back to the woman; the resemblance was uncanny! Somewhere in my mind, a question was formulating; and as it made its way from my brain, down the millions of nerve endings that worked my vocal cords, my heart began to beat a million times a second…. "What is your name?" I asked. The lady turned to me and said, "My name? My name is Emelia." I asked, "Emelia Postrell?" She looked at me curiously. "Did you have a sister that went to America to study by the name of Kalana Postrell?" Emelia sat motionless and said, "Yes, how did you know my sister?" I think it's best if we let this lady tell the story. (I pointed to Sister.) For the next two hours, we sat as Sister told her story from the dreams, the hunt for Ethell Gush and the treachery that had been bestowed upon the Postrell family in America. When Sister completed her story, Ms. Postrell was emotional. She asked, "So, are you trying to tell me that all this time, my beautiful niece, my sibling's only child, has been alive and been alone for all these years?" Emelia began to weep and continued, "You have no idea how close I was to my sister. She was my older and only sibling. It was just the two of us. I loved her with all my heart. When we heard of her passing, we immediately flew to America to claim her body and to bring her child home. But when we got there, we were told that not only had she died, but also the child had died as well. We mourned for her for months on end. Some of us are still in mourning. We claimed both bodies and flew them back here. Both are buried in our family plot. I was so grieved that I pledged never to marry and to never have children; because we had promised to get married on the same day and have children that would grow up together. If you are willing to take a DNA test and it proves you to be who you say you are, then you will claim what is your mother's property. But I already know who you are. Until the DNA test comes back, I want you all to stay at my villa." I leaned over to Kendral and whispered, "Did she just say villa?" She made some phone calls and we ended up at a hospital where blood samples of Sister and Ms. Postrell were taken. The test would not be back for a few days. After that we hopped another cab, and we headed for a twenty-mile ride to the Hilbram District. Along the way, my mind was trying to figure out something. The Consulate director had said that Sister was probably related to the field hands by her skin complexion, which was very light. Yet Ms. Postrell's complexion was very dark. Indian blood lines are strictly held, so how did Sister become so light skinned? We drove until we came up to a tall wall with a huge steel gate. We noticed a family crescent rested above the gate. A guard opened the gate and we slowly drove into the villa.

You would not believe the lush beauty of the yards! Outside the gate was a dry desert landscape but once entering the villa, there were all colors of flowers in bloom and large yards of beautiful green grasses. Colorful flowers hung from terraces and water fountains bubbled. The front of the villa had a large beautifully handcrafted double door. Two spiral staircases ran from the top floor down to the front yard. As we pulled up, several maids came out to meet us. They treated us like royalty! On our way up to the door, I questioned Sister about what the man had said about the family skin tones. She told me that her father's father was "Mulatto". That answered my question. Her real mother was as dark as the night sky and her dad was as brown as a Buster Brown shoe. From the photo of him on her wall, she wasn't far off. I had often wondered why her skin complexion was light. She had gained the light gene from her grandfather! After climbing several flights of stairs, we finally arrived at our rooms.

The rooms were so beautiful! It was like staying in a five-star hotel. Once again, I was feeling that "I'm on vacation feeling." Sister and Ms. Postrell spent the next several days alone. We spent the next several days walking the villa and taking horse driven carriages out to the coffee and tea fields. The landscape behind the villa was breathtaking. The carriage driver told us that the Postrells owned three thousand acres of prime farmland. They contracted out directly to the government and the military. The government chose which crops were grown each year. If Sister was part of this family, she was into some serious money! Three glorious days passed. We had been in prayer every night hoping that Sister's journey had come to a beautiful end. On the fourth day we were summoned to meet back downstairs at 7:30 that evening in the large eating hall. When we got to the room, it had been decorated festively. About twenty people sat at the large dining table. Servants guided us to our places. There were three seats not yet filled. One empty seat was at the head and the other two were on either side of it. Then from out of a side room, Ms. Postrell came in but did not sit at the head of the table. That confused us. Then from another door, Sister came in... and did she look beautiful! She was dressed in a very expensive Indian attire that screamed royalty and power. She wore it with a smile and a blush. As she was headed to the other side chair, maids quickly ran up to her and guided her to the head of the table. I was curious as to why they did that; but I guess that's how they treated their honored guest. Even if she had been related to them, surely, they would not have put her at the head of the table. I could see on Sister's face that she was just as surprised as we were that she was being seated there. What we did not realize at the time, was that Sister was actually the second highest-ranking member of the family and was being honored as such. Then, Ms. Postrell stood, clinking a fork on a glass, and said, "I would like for you all to meet Palma Postrell, daughter and only child of my late sister, Kalana Postrell. In the Indian culture, the oldest child is given the lion's share of the parent's holdings. "In my sister's absence, I was the only heir; so, all the shares fell to me. I have no children. If my older sister was still here today and she was passing away, her share would pass to her child. You now see that child sitting at the head of the table. She has come to claim what is rightfully hers. Now before you, at this table, is every member of this family who can dispute this claim. The facts are that through DNA testing, this is my sister's child. If there is anyone here today who wants to challenge this, then let him or her speak now." There was silence. Everyone waited for someone to challenge. The challenge never came; but what did come was the sound of a chair sliding from the table, and a man stood. He walked away from his chair, and I thought he was about to walk out. Instead, he walked around the table, grabbed Ms. Postrell's hand and kissed it. Then he took from his pocket a small metal container that looked like a makeup tin. He put one of his fingers in the tin and gently swirled his finger around in it. He then turned to Sister and with his hand, he raised her chin high and took his finger and rubbed a red circle on her forehead. Then he kissed her on both cheeks and said, "Welcome home, Palma!" The whole crowd began to clap. I thought to myself, "This is like a living fairytale and we are part of it." We celebrated that night. We gave Sister plenty of room to meet her family. I thought to myself "From nothing she came, but to all she gained!" Then unexpectedly, Ms. Postrell began clicking the side of her glass with a spoon to get everyone's attention. "May I have your undivided attention please. Palma has something that she has to say." Sister, already standing by her aunt, began to say, "I want you all to understand something that is very important to me. I do not know your religious beliefs here, but I want you to clearly understand mine. I am a Christian, first and foremost. I will not serve or participate in anything that might offend my God. You, of course, can do as you like. I have to give honor to my God in all things. I give Him all the honor, glory and praise; and He and He alone get the credit for what has transpired here. But to you, I give thanks for allowing the spirit of love and honor to overcome any doubts or mistrust. From servant to family, I will always have your best interest at my heart, because I want to; but more importantly, because I am commanded to by my Lord and Savior, who is Jesus Christ." There was silence. The crowd seemed good with that. So, all together, Kendral, Momma, and I raised our glasses and said, "Amen!" Later that night, Sister summoned us to her room. Her room was so large. It felt like we walked into a house within a house. Sister began to explain why Mrs. Postrell was calling her, Palma, instead of Sarah. Sarah was the name on her American birth certificate. She began with the "Palma Postrell" name. "Before I was born, I was already given a name. As teens, my mother and my Aunt had already dreamed of being married and having children. They even went as far as naming their children they had not conceived yet. I was, "Palma" way before I was, "Sarah". It's dated and written in the family's historical book. I am told on my supposed grave, somewhere on this property, there are two names, Kalana Postrell and daughter Palma Postrell." Sister continued and told us that she is the rightful co-owner of a business called Delightful Farms. It is the largest owner operated farm in India. According to last year's profits, the farm makes several millions of dollars a year. Our mouths hung open like empty caves. Kendral asked, "So where do you go from here?" She replied, "I will stay here with my real family; and you will go back to America and live your lives that are waiting for you there. There is nothing left there for me. I will contact my kids and inform them of what has transpired thus far; and I will leave it up to them as to what they want to do. I will keep in touch with you; because to be honest, you guys are a part of this family just as much as my kids are." The last night at the villa was sad; but I found some comfort in knowing that Sister's life was now fully complete.

We returned to America and with a spirit lifting adventure under our belt, we continued to be encouraged. The boring life we had previously led was forever gone. Just as she had promised, twice a year on the exact same day of every year, we received a letter from Sister. Often the letter was a simple catch up on reconstructions at the villa; but every now and then, she would remember or forget some small detail about the adventure we had shared together, and she would ask about that. In February of 2011, we received that year's first letter from India. But this time, the letter included plane tickets. We had been requested by the very aging aunt, Ms. Postrell, to come to India. The letter informed us that Sister had become ill and was not doing well. A week later, we landed in India and were off to the villa. When we got there, we were greeted by her family and her children. We were worried about Sister's health so we immediately asked whether we could see her. The maids motioned us into the big house, and I noticed one of Sister's children began to tear up. This gave me a really bad feeling, but I kept quiet. We were led down a few stairs below ground through a narrow hall. When we entered the room, and after seeing what lay before us, I began to repeat softly, "O, no" with tears running down my eyes. There was a glass covered coffin on a huge, beautiful cedar table. In it lay our beloved Sister in magnificent attire. The room became full of despair and deep sympathy fell like a fog. I think I took it the worst. Kendral seemed to be in a distant place, so that the shock of her passing away did not consume him. Momma was on her knees in repeated chants of "No, no. It can't be, not my beloved Sister!" Then Ms. Postrell said in a solemn voice, "Things happened quickly. She kept secrets from us all. The doctors told me they didn't understand why we could not tell she was ill. I guess with her profound strength and will she hid everything from us. The night she lay down, we had just spent a whole day working in the flower garden and later that night we entertained some guests from Ghana. She showed no sign of weakness. Between the wigs and makeup, she kept her illness hidden. The doctors claimed she knew that she had been sick for over six years before coming to India. So, all that time she was looking for us, she was also dealing with her illness. The few years I had to spend with her will be my life's greatest memory."

Sister was buried on a large hill on the property. Dignitaries and people of all influences attended her funeral. They spared no money to make her funeral an event to remember! We had front row access to Sister's body during the funeral. Ms. Postrell made it very clear to the family how important we had been to Sister; so, everyone moved aside for us. Before they closed the lid on her coffin, the four of us, including Ms. Postrell, walked to view Sister's body one last time. I reached out and touched Sister's hand. Immediately I had an open vision. The vision was of Sister, with a red pearl on her forehead and in one motion, she flung out her arms toward me and opened her hands. All sorts of beautiful exotic flowers were slung towards me. It seemed like every color of the rainbow was represented. As she did that she said, "So that you will never forget." I must have passed out because I awoke lying in bed. Kendral was patting my forehead with a wet cool towel. I tried to get up, but he gently held me down and said, "Whoa, take it easy. You passed out today. The doctors said you are in perfect health; but you are a little dehydrated, which led to your passing out." Momma was on the other side of the bed looking like a soldier guarding a precious jewel. She asked, "Are you alright Kitty?" I nodded my head and continued to pan the room, as Kendral put more pillows under my head. Once I realized that no one else was in the room, I said, "Sister spoke to me from the coffin. That is why I passed out. The contact was so strong and so vivid that it overwhelmed me. She left us a message." I took a swallow of the water Momma was putting to my mouth. When I then told them what I had seen, they pondered on the vision. After all we had been through with the adventure and considering how vivid the dream was, it led us to believe that Sister had left some valuable information that we had not gotten yet, as a gift to our friendship. After a little more rest, I awoke fresh and fully recovered. It was 5:30 Friday evening.

The day had been a particularly hot one with temperatures soaring to triple digits. The villa buildings were made from stucco and a mud compact composite material, which easily kept the buildings cooled. Kendral had lay down beside me in bed and was snoring away; and Momma was stretched out on a sofa. A knock at the door brought all of us out of our sleep. "Come in," I answered. The butler of the house walked two steps into the room and said, "You are all requested to meet in the East Dining Room at 7:30 pm sharp tonight. Lady Postrell has invited the other major family members to hear Sister's last will and testament." Without saying anything else, the butler took two identical steps backwards, grabbed the doorknob and shut the door. Kendral said, "That dude needs to loosen up a bit." Taking his attention off the now closed door, he asked. "You don't reckon the old girl left us something, do you?" He turned to me and Momma wearing a smirk on his face. We both shrugged and I was off to take a shower. It was now 7:20 and there was a knock at the door. The butler said through the door, "First and last call." We were dressed and found our way to the room. It was magnificently decorated. Tassels and draperies hung from the ceilings with large crystal chandeliers giving brilliant lighting. Around the whole room stood formally dressed maids, as If the President of the United States was arriving. As the people began to pour in, an announcer introduced who they were and how they were connected to Sister. Afterwards, maids began to seat each person in prearranged seats. At least 25 people had already seated, I guess we would be seated last. The announcer said, "Hailing from the America's, the closest, dearest and most loyal friends of Lady Palma: her Staff, (he motioned to Kendral) her Pen, (he motioned to me) and her Whip, (he motioned to Momma). Ladies and gentlemen, I would like for you to meet Sir Ken, Lady Kathy, and Elder Celia." I questioned to no one quietly, "We had titles now?" The whole room stood and clapped as we were seated, not at the end of the table but at the head. We were taken off guard by this, but we managed. After the applause, Ms. Postrell came in with a short man that had a briefcase. He sat to Ms. Postrell's right, cleared his throat and said in an old English accent, "By the power of attorney invested and trusted to me by the late Mrs. Palma and the state of India, I am hereby taking liberty to read the late Palma Postrell's last will and testament and amendment thereof." I glanced at Kendral and Momma, as both of their eyebrows raised, and Kendral leaned to me and asked, "Amendment, and where are the kids?" The man, who I perceived to be a lawyer, proceeded to open his briefcase and thus he said… "The children of Lady Palma's have already been given their portion of the allocated estate left by Lady Palma and have returned to the Americas. That being said, all of her assets, that were not a part of the family business, they were entitled to, they have taken. As far as the family business, they have no physical power in the family business as per the saying of the will and according to the family's strict rules. They may live on her property, but the property will always remain in the Postrells name and in the Postrells complete control. The children will get a yearly financial allotment, which is already assigned to each of them to do with as they wish." With that he grabbed his glass of water, took a sip, wiped his eyeglasses to a perfect shine, and began opening a second folded sheet of paper. The man cleared his throat and looked towards us and said, "Now to the amendment that I do attest, as a witness and a cosigner, that herein and herewith out but cannot be challenged under any government or any family entity. He began to read. "On August 12, 2011, I, Palma Postrell, hereby granted by way of power endowed to me by the Postrell's name that the three sitting before you are indeed my family. It is not legal to give any lands of India to any person who is not a citizen of the Indian citizenship; therefore, I was unable to accomplish that. But nonetheless, our Lord and Savior will still be Glorified. (There was a slight shift in body languages around the table as people struggled with the term Lord and Savior, for they were all Hindus). To Kendral, Kathy, and Ceil, I hereby leave a portion. A portion that somehow, I pray cultivates the love I have for the three. Every year, for as long as they may live, one million dollars shall be deposited into an American account on January 1st of each year. Then the bank shall divide to each of the three an equal share of that million." I looked around the table at her family; and everyone was stone faced and looking at the lawyer. Was I the only one at this table ready to cry and scream for joy? Momma didn't help any; because she looked like she had just seen the ending of a movie with a cliffhanger. But Kendral saved me. His grin started at the middle of his face and ran all the way up to his ears! The lawyer looked around the table reading himself for any objection, none came so he continued. "Also, it is Lady Palma's desire that the names of these three be added to the family tree.... This is the wish she asked of her family." There were nods all around the table. Tears were running down my cheeks. Kendral was softly patting me on the back and Momma was awed at the large painting being uncovered behind us on the wall. It was a huge mural of her family tree, going back four hundred years! Towards the bottom of the tree was Sister's name; and below her to the right were her children; but immediately to her left read, "My Friends: Kathy, Kendral, and Ceil." I began to cry all over again. The room was solemn, but I was torn to my heart. Kendral had even begun to cry, and Momma was on her knees at the wall.

It's been two years since that day. A lingering question remains... Why did Sister decide to keep her illness a secret? After all, we were in a prayer group together, in which many times we prayed for people that were ill. We would like to believe that Sister had already dealt with God on this issue, and she had accepted His answer. Whatever the truth may be, the fact is, the choice was hers and hers alone. Sister's children have never contacted us. Every now and then, we get a postcard from Ms.

Postrell. There is never a day that goes by when we don't think about our beloved Sister. Sometimes we drive by her old house and reminisce.

Momma, Kendral, and I were eating breakfast one morning at the local Huddle House, when a man walked up to the table. We recognized him immediately. It was none other than Mr. Late Evening. He sat and I was about to say hello, when he put a finger to his lips and said, "Shhh." He looked around and leaned in and said, "I need your help!" Kendral looked toward me and Momma and said, "O boy, here we go again!"

The End

EPILOGUE

*I*t is amazing to look back on our life seeing God working in it. He orchestrated this incredible time we shared with one of the most interesting persons we have ever met. This book was an idea that brought closure to her life and completeness to ours. When she passed away, she left behind her the only three people who truly knew her and believed in her. Our lives were brought together by God and God alone. There is no other way to explain it. He was the glue that bound us together and kept us honest with one another. The reason we believed in her almost unbelievable story was simply an act of God, I can't say that enough. From the very beginning, her dire hopeless situation, reflected on our own. We dared to believe in a dream that for some part became a reality. In the end, I am left with asking myself questions beyond her grave. "Sister, what are you up to now? Are you behaving or are you arguing with Moses about why he never entered the Promised Land?" I pray though, that you are resting; but knowing you, I doubt it. We have written this story, 'So that we will never forget!' Love you always, Kathy, Kendral, and Ceil.

Printed in the United States
by Baker & Taylor Publisher Services